The Mini Farming Guide to Vegetable Gardening

The Mini Farming Guide to Vegetable Gardening

Self-Sufficiency from Asparagus to Zucchini

Brett L. Markham

Skyhorse Publishing

Skyhorse Publishing books may be purchased in bulk at special discounts for sales promotion, corporate gifts, fund-raising, or educational purposes. Special editions can also be created to specifications. For details, contact the Special Sales Department, Skyhorse Publishing, 307 West 36th Street, 11th Floor, New York, NY 10018 or info@skyhorsepublishing.com.

Skyhorse® and Skyhorse Publishing® are registered trademarks of Skyhorse Publishing, Inc.®, a Delaware corporation.

Visit our website at www.skyhorsepublishing.com

10 9 8 7 6 5 4 3 2 1

Library of Congress Cataloging-in-Publication Data is available on file.

ISBN: 978-1-61608-615-2

Printed in China

Contents

Acknowledgments and Dedication

When you work a full-time job doing something other than writing, the time you do spend writing necessarily takes away from other activities. And those other activities usually involve other people: friends, family, colleagues, and loved ones who sacrifice access to your time and attention so you can write. Too many people to list have sacrificed so that I could write, so here I would like to acknowledge my thanks and appreciation to each and every one of them for their kindness and forbearance.

I have also received a lot of encouragement from a diverse group of people who would certainly seem strange bedfellows at first glance, but beneath the surface share important commonalities. I have received encouragement from people interested in self-sufficiency, people concerned about the environment and peak oil, nutrition activists, permaculturists, political activists encompassing everything from anarchists and libertarians to the far right and more. In the long run, all human life starts from the soil, so it isn't surprising that such a diverse group of sincerely caring people, despite superficial differences, would share a common understanding of the importance of our bond to the soil and the value of food self-sufficiency. I appreciate all of the encouragement I have received from all of these fine people.

Skyhorse Publishing took a big financial risk in putting my ideas to print. Printing books is an expensive enterprise, and the risk of holding untold numbers of unwanted books is quite real. You can go to many job-lot type stores and find tens of thousands of unsold books marked down to under a dollar—well under the cost of printing—just to get rid of them. It is easy to forget, looking at the phenomenal success that *Mini Farming* has become, that publishing it in the first place was to some extent an act of faith in an unproven author. And to some degree, Skyhorse's willingness to publish this book as well is a risk. Though I realize it is a risk that holds the potential for the company to more than recoup its investments, I am nevertheless appreciative of the fact Skyhorse continues to publish my work, and especially for the fact the company gives me carte blanche without trying to micromanage my subject matter.

There are many more people I could and perhaps should acknowledge for the role they play or have played in making this book and my others possible. No man is an island, and to varying degrees we all reflect the influences of others in our lives. But because this is a down-and-dirty, nuts-and-bolts book aimed not at the theory of mini farming but at its actual practice, I would like to dedicate this book to a very special group of people: Those Who Do.

Foreword:
Why Grow Your
Own Vegetables?

According to an article in the *Journal of the American Medical Association*,[1] medical errors are the third leading cause of death in the United States. Deaths result from unnecessary surgery, dose-dependent adverse drug reactions, superbug infections, and more. So even though I am not a medical doctor, I believe I am sufficiently qualified to reiterate our mothers' collective wisdom that we ought to eat our vegetables, if for no other reason than to prevent as much contact as possible with the medical community.

There is no dietary component with a greater effect than vegetables. The more vegetables in your diet, the longer and

---

1   Starfield, B. (2000), *Journal of the American Medical Association* Vol. 284, July 26, 2000

more healthy your life, and the fewer the vegetables in your diet, the shorter and less healthy your life. It's really that simple. Study after study demonstrates that vegetables contain hundreds of important compounds to fight or prevent practically all chronic diseases, and links vegetable consumption with lower incidence of disease even in cases in which other adverse lifestyle practices are present.

Unfortunately, it isn't that simple in daily practice for two reasons. Vegetables are expensive because they are labor-intensive to produce, and quite often they are tasteless or downright unappealing when available because of the results of modern agricultural practices.

At first glance, fresh (or at least not cooked) vegetables don't look that expensive. You can get broccoli florets for $4 per pound, cabbage for $3 per head, and tomatoes for $1.69 each. These prices don't look so bad until you realize just how many vegetables you should be eating.

Even when the USDA nutritional guidelines were five half-cup servings (about two pounds) of vegetables daily, fewer than 10 percent of Americans consumed that many vegetables. In addition, those guidelines are based upon the USDA recommended daily allowance (RDA) for various nutrients. The RDA for nutrients is sufficient to avoid obvious symptoms of deficiency, but according to many researchers and scientists, is insufficient to convey optimal health or prevent chronic diseases.[2]

Though it is possible to augment nutrient intake with vitamin pills, it is widely recognized that vitamin pills are inferior to food sources because foods convey the vitamins along with a wide array of other nutrients that can't be duplicated in a pill. These other nutrients augment the effects of the vitamins and also provide their own unique benefits. In order to obtain a level of nutrients for optimal health, you'd have to eat ten half-cup servings of a variety of fruits and vegetables daily. This amounts to four pounds of vegetables.

If you have four people in your family and each requires a modest three pounds a day of vegetables, that comes out to twelve pounds a day or eighty-four pounds a week. Even at $4 a pound for conventionally farmed produce, that creates a $336/week grocery bill for vegetables alone. This is one reason why nutritional levels are so bad in poorer communities and why even middle-class Americans consume vegetables more as an afterthought or as an adjunct than as a primary food source.

---

2   Orthomolecular News Service, October 30, 2007, "Doctors Say, Raise the RDAs Now"

Vegetables are nutrient-dense, but they are not calorie-dense. Calorie for calorie, vegetables are substantially more expensive than other common foods.

Compare, for example, sirloin steak at $7 per pound and 74 calories per ounce to cabbage at $1.69 per pound and 6.4 calories per ounce. With steak you get 168 calories per dollar, whereas with cabbage you get 60 calories per dollar. Steak and cabbage are both healthful foods, but matters get even worse when comparing unhealthful foods such as candy or snack chips to vegetables. A 3 1/4-ounce package of a popular candy costs only 89 cents but packs 240 calories, providing 270 calories per dollar. This comparative cost per calorie is one reason why vegetables provide fewer than 10 percent of the calories in the average American's diet. Even though organic vegetables are more healthful and tasty for a variety of reasons, they are even less likely to provide many calories in the average diet because they are more expensive than conventional vegetables on a per-calorie basis.

When you grow your own vegetables, you can grow them far less expensively than they can be purchased, thereby making it much more feasible to follow our mothers' advice.

Another reason why people don't eat enough vegetables, I am sad to say, is because most vegetables you can buy at the supermarket are unappetizing. Humans have a natural evolutionary desire to consume the most calorie-dense food available in order to avoid starvation. To a degree, this can explain our preference for snack cakes over rutabagas. But another important ingredient in that equation is that industrial agriculture has turned what should be a culinary delight into something so tasteless and useless that it can't be consumed in quantity without a dip or sauce to disguise its bland character.

Modern farming is as close to an industrial process as practicable. Like any other commercial enterprise, especially one whose products are traded on a commodity market, the drive is to get produce to market with the lowest possible costs. Human health and nutrition are not factors.

I am reminded of a recent trip to an auto dealership where I traded in a truck. I had recently invested in a new steering box, had always used synthetic oil, and had overall maintained the truck flawlessly. It ran well, and it should have. But as a trade-in on the commodity market of used vehicles, it was worth the exact same price as if it wouldn't run, it had been poorly maintained, and the engine had been removed. I am exaggerating a bit for effect, but that is what goes on. So, given that, what is my motivation to put serious money into maintaining a truck when it is treated identically to much more poorly maintained vehicles when traded in?

Well, my motivation is straightforward: the truck was primarily for my own use, and as such my own comfort and safety hinged on keeping the truck in good repair. The car dealership deals in a commodity. Any extra value added to what you place on the product is lost because everything is priced to the lowest common denominator. But when it is for your own use, that value is never really lost because of the value you personally derive from the investment.

The agribusiness sector is no different. You can go to a commodity market and place a bid for bushels of corn, pork bellies, or tomatoes. There isn't a place to put your bid on "Brett's vine-ripened organic tomatoes lovingly grown in a soil rich in micronutrients." My tomatoes are far better tasting and dramatically more healthful than those traded on the market, but if I am going to get paid the same for them as if I had slathered them with poison and grown them in toxic waste, from a purely dollars and cents perspective, it is most economically efficient for me to use slave labor, grow them in toxic waste, and coat them with every poison under the sun.

As a result, the vegetables that are available for you to purchase at the super-market are overwhelmingly horrible. Its no wonder that nobody wants to eat them! Even worse, their nutrient levels have declined dramatically. For example, broccoli has 37 percent less calcium than it did in 1950, and squash has 52 percent less riboflavin. This same pattern repeats for a variety of nutrients across a spectrum of forty-three garden crops tested.[3] Vegetables are still more healthful than snack cakes, but they are a lot less healthful than they used to be.

I grew up in rural southwestern Virginia in an area most would consider "the middle of nowhere." As a result, homegrown vegetables were the norm. When I left home and moved to the Northeast, I was seriously shocked at how horrible most vegetables tasted. I had no idea that the food available in supermarkets was of such poor quality. Oh sure, it is *visually* appealing, but taste buds reveal the illusion.

You may have heard of Linux. Linux is a computer operating system that is licensed under something called the GNU Public License (GPL). The first Linux kernel was developed by Linus Torvalds in 1991, and released under the GPL. Today, the majority of servers on the Internet are running some variant of Linux and a great deal of the core infrastructure uses software released under the GPL.

---

3   Davis, D., Epp, M., Riordan, H. (2004), "Changes in USDA food composition data for 43 garden crops" *J Am Coll Nutr* December 2004 vol. 23 no. 6 669-682

The GPL was invented by Richard Stallman, who founded the Free Software Foundation. The idea behind GPL was to make software that anyone could work on and modify in order to enhance its capabilities or fix bugs. This stood in contrast to the existing proprietary system in which the users of software were utterly dependent on the suppliers.

Richard Stallman's motivation in creating the open source idea was, in his words, to create "software that doesn't suck." Now, if you search for that phrase on a search engine, you will get tens of thousands of hits. The idea of allowing the end user of software to modify it took off and has led to increasingly feature-rich and robust software. Open-source software has even created a motivation for the creators of proprietary software to improve the quality and openness of their offerings.

To paraphrase Richard Stallman within the context of food, another important reason to grow your own vegetables is so you can grow "food that doesn't suck." When you grow your own vegetables, you can grow the most tasty varieties in nutrient-rich soils, and you can allow them to ripen naturally so they can be harvested at their nutritional peak. You have the power to grow vegetables that you and your family will actually look forward to eating, rather than hiding them under a sauce or cooking them to death just to get them out of the way.

And you can also take part in a gardening version of GPL by growing open-pollinated varieties of vegetables from which you can save your own seeds and become independent of some faceless corporation half a world away. In so doing, you can adapt varieties to your own conditions and needs, thereby making them the best they can possibly be.

Yet another reason to grow your own vegetables is a moral one. I am not about to stand on a soapbox and start telling you how to live your life. Rather, I am already confident that we share certain basic moral views, but that overall our media has done a very poor job of telling you what is going on today in agribusiness. All I am going to do is inform you of certain facts. I'm certain that this will be sufficient.

I was a child when Ronald Reagan was president and he initiated the so-called "War on Drugs." I am not personally a big fan of the war on drugs, but something he said in a speech stuck with me and guaranteed I would never even try an illegal drug. He explained that at various places in the supply chain of drugs there was a culture of heinous violence, murder, and wanton disregard for human life, and that by purchasing drugs I would be contributing to that system.

Whether or not drugs should be illegal or there should be a war on drugs at all is not the point. The point is that right now, as things stand, people die every day in violence tied to the trafficking of drugs; and if I buy those drugs I am contributing to that culture of violence. If you want to use them, that's none of my business, incidentally. I'm just explaining why *I* don't.

So why am I talking about that? The media has done a very poor job of informing you that human slavery is so intimately involved in the production of fruits and vegetables that if you go buy produce at the supermarket, it is certain that your hands will touch produce that has touched the hand of a slave.

I am not using the terms "slave" and "slavery" as hyperbole and I am not taking literary license. I am not speaking of "slavery-like" conditions, poor wages, long hours, or bad housing. Rather, I am talking about honest to goodness slavery in which human beings are sold on the auction block, bound in chains, beaten if they are too sick to work, and even shot when they try to run away. And I am talking about it happening right here, in the United States.

Though the practices are ubiquitous, they are hard to prosecute in a realm where employers are legally allowed to employ isolated, non-English-speaking migrant labor at low wages and house them in substandard conditions. It can be hard, also, to know who exactly is the slaveholder. There have been seven successful prosecutions of agricultural slaveholders in Florida in just the past fifteen years. Unfortunately, it is hard to prove "who knew what and when they knew it," so those prosecuted are usually underlings whose conditions are hardly better than those of the slaves. Even so, Chief Assistant U.S. Attorney Douglas Molloy has stated that the tomato growing region of Florida is "ground zero for modern slavery."[4]

Journalist Barry Estabrook, in recounting an interview with Douglas Molloy reports as follows:[5]

"When I asked Molloy if it was safe to assume that a consumer who has eaten a tomato from a grocery store, fast-food restaurant, or food-service company in the winter has eaten a fruit picked by the hand of a slave, he corrected my choice of words. 'It's not an assumption. It is a fact.'"

So another good reason to grow your own vegetables is to reduce the level of financial support you provide to a system of modern slavery. Slavery is driven by

---

4   Estabrook, B. (2009), "Politics of the Plate: The Price of Tomatoes," *Gourmet*, March 2009
5   Estabrook, B. (2011), *Tomatoland*, Andrews McMeel Publishing, LLC

economic factors, and by reducing consumption of goods produced via slavery, you reduce the economic incentive for slavery. In the past dozen years, police have freed more than a thousand agricultural workers in Florida who were kept captive and threatened with death if they tried to escape.[6] But that is just the tip of the iceberg, and by growing as much of our own produce as possible, people with no police powers at all can have a far greater effect in eliminating slavery on this continent.

So, I believe I have given you some really compelling reasons for growing your own vegetables. Doing so is less expensive and will improve your health, the vegetables you grow will be tastier and hold more nutrients, and you will help end slavery.

This book is a follow-up to my earlier book *Mini Farming: Self-Sufficiency on ¼ Acre*. In that book, I explain composting, the timing of planting and harvesting, establishing beds, canning, dehydrating, and much more. I even explain cover cropping, crop rotation, how to make your own organic fertilizers, and how to make your own chicken plucker. *Mini Farming* contains a lot of information, and in this book, I assume (hopefully correctly!) that you have already read that book or have a copy handy.

After *Mini Farming* was published, I started getting a lot of crop-specific questions via my website. "How do I prune an indeterminate tomato?" "Can I grow winter squash on a trellis?" I want to answer all of those questions in this book.

I hope my publisher isn't cringing too badly, but ethics are important in this world. Most of this book, excepting the introduction and the chapter on perennial vegetables, is excerpted from a longer and more involved book titled *Maximizing Your Mini-Farm*. That book contains all of the same information as you'll find in this one, along with instructions on making a number of helpful garden tools, wine, vinegar, and cheese. If you are only interested in vegetables then this book is a better choice for you than *Maximizing*.

Both books are worthwhile in my opinion and ideal for their respective target audiences, and I believe they will benefit their readers or I wouldn't have bothered. But if I'm going to tell you how to save money, that can start by helping you decide what to buy so you don't make a duplicate purchase.

The material in this book is directly or indirectly the result of questions from the readers of *Mini Farming*. I would like to thank everyone who has read *Mini*

---

6   PBS (2009) Update: Tomatoes of Wrath, March 13, 2009

Farming and also those who asked questions to help me clarify the thoughts you'll find in these pages. Happy farming!

Brett L. Markham
New Ipswich, New Hampshire
September 2011

The Mini Farming Guide to Vegetable Gardening

1

Soil and Fertility

In Mini Farming: *Self-Sufficiency on ¼ Acre,* I spent several chapters discussing soil and fertility in depth. The reason is because proper soil management and fertility practices are the foundation upon which everything else is built to make mini farming an economically viable enterprise rather than merely a hobby. Optimum soil leads to reduced problems with pests and diseases, supports higher yields with greater density, creates more nutritious food, and allows you to spend less money and effort on getting more food.

In this chapter, I am going to summarize what you need to know, plus add a bit more information. This summary should be enough to get you started, though it doesn't substitute for the in-depth knowledge in *Mini Farming: Self-Sufficiency on ¼ Acre.*

Raised Beds

I recommend planting in raised beds for a number of important reasons. Raised beds that have been double-dug and enriched with finished compost retain water while properly draining so that oxygen levels in the soil are optimal, nutrients are bound in a living symbiotic matrix for release to plants as needed, and soil temperatures allow for early working. Furthermore, the close spacing of plants in a raised bed increases yields over use of row gardening while growing closely enough together to shade out weeds.

Beds are also useful for practicing crop rotation on a small scale. Every crop has slightly different requirements and places slightly different demands on the soil as well as enhancing it in different ways. Probably the single most dangerous thing that can be done, in terms of pests and disease, is growing the same crop in the same place year after year. By doing this, diseases and pests build up until they are ultimately beyond control. Rotating crops between beds substantially reduces pest and disease problems.

In general, beds should be placed near each other, but with enough space to walk between them. The space between the beds can be sod/grass, crushed stones, bark mulch, or practically anything else. Usually, sod/grass is not a problem, and that is what is between my beds. However, these can serve as a reservoir for diseases such as botrytis and a breeding ground for wireworms while providing easy access to slugs; so if disease problems are experienced or wireworms start doing serious damage, using (untreated) bark mulch or straw between the beds to suppress grasses may be wise. Also, if any grass isn't mowed regularly, it can grow over into a bed. The next thing you know, you'll be pulling grass out of your beds by the handful.

Composting

Composting is the key to preserving and enhancing the fertility of the soil. The law of conservation of matter says that matter cannot be created or destroyed. Without getting into the physics of matter/energy systems, in practical terms this means that the elements in a plant came from the soil, and unless those elements are put back into the soil, a mini farmer will find it necessary to purchase outside inputs such as fertilizer. Thus, if the foliage of a tomato plant has taken phosphorus from the soil and that plant is simply discarded, the phosphorus will need to be replenished from an outside source. But if, instead, that plant is composted, the phosphorus can then be returned to the soil via the compost and thereby reduce the need for an outside source of phosphorus.

Compost is a complex and literally living substance made from the aerobic decomposition of organic matter. Other than volatile elements such as nitrogen, all of the essential elements added to the pile as part of the composted materials are retained. But, in addition, the process of composting breaks down poisons, destroys both human and plant pathogens, generates a wide array of beneficial soil organisms that help plants get the most from the nutrients in the soil, and even produces antibiotics for combating diseases.

Composting, therefore, is absolutely crucial from an economic perspective because of the way it reduces the need for fertilizers; it also serves to passively prevent a whole host of pest and disease problems. The importance of composting cannot be overemphasized. You should be adding at least four cubic feet of finished compost to every 4 ft. x 8 ft. bed annually.

pH

The pH is a measure of how acidic or alkaline the soil is. It is important because plants generally have a certain range of pH preference for optimal growth and because the pH of the soil actively affects which microorganisms will thrive in the environment and how readily the nutrients contained in the soil can be used by plants. The pH is measured on a scale from 0 to 14. Zero (0) is highly acidic like battery acid; 14 is highly basic like lye; and 7 is neutral.

Many sources list a pH preference range for each plant, but these sources often differ in the details. For example, one source will list the preferred pH for tomatoes as 5.8 to 6.5, whereas another will list it as 6 to 7. The simple fact is that you don't need to be that detailed, as with only a very few exceptions, plants grown for food in gardens will grow well with a pH ranging from 6 to 7. True, a cucumber can grow at a pH as high as 8, but it will also grow at 6.5.

Because pH corrections can take months to show results and because the constant rotation of beds between crops makes it impractical to customize the pH of a bed to a given crop, it makes sense to test each bed individually, and correct the beds to a uniform pH of between 6 and 6.5. The exceptions are that the beds used for potatoes should have the pH lower than this, and the beds used for brassicas (such as cabbage and broccoli) should have extra lime added to the holes where the transplants are placed. These practices will be specifically covered in the chapters pertaining to those particular plants.

In most of the country, the soil pH is too low and needs to be raised to be within an optimal range. Correcting pH using lime can be problematic in that it takes several months to act. Though the gardening year should start in the fall along with any soil corrections so the lime has time to react with the soil, the reality of life is that the decision to start a garden is generally made in late winter or early spring. Thus, the farmer is stuck trying to correct pH within weeks of planting instead of months. However, with a bit of creativity and the use of alternate materials, both short- and long-term corrections can be made to the pH.

There are many liming materials available for this purpose but only four I would recommend: powdered lime, pelleted lime, dolomitic lime, and wood ashes. Others such as burnt and hydrated lime act more quickly, but are hazardous to handle and easy to overapply. If you choose to use these latter products, please follow package directions closely.

Pelleted lime is powdered lime that has been mixed with an innocuous water-soluble adhesive for ease of spreading. It acts no more or less quickly than the powdered product but costs more. Lime can take as long as a year to take full effect, but it will remain effective for as long as seven years.

Dolomitic lime contains magnesium in place of some of the calcium. In most soils in the U.S. (excepting clay soils in the Carolinas), using dolomitic lime for up to one quarter of the liming is beneficial to supply needed magnesium with calcium. It is used at the same rate as regular lime, takes as long to act, and lasts as long.

Wood ashes are a long-neglected soil amendment for pH correction. They contain a wide array of macronutrients such as potassium and calcium but also contain elements such as iron, boron, and copper. They act more quickly in correcting soil pH but do not last as long. Wood ashes are applied at twice the rate of lime for an equal pH correction but should not be applied at a rate exceeding five pounds per 100 square feet. So, in effect, wood ashes are always used in conjunction with lime rather than on their own.

The pH scale is a logarithmic value, similar to a decibel. As such, the amount of lime needed to raise the pH from 4 to 5 is greater than the amount of lime needed to raise the pH from 5 to 6. Furthermore, the effectiveness of lime is strongly influenced by the type of soil. So the following table reflects both of these factors. The numbers represent pounds of powdered limestone per 100 square feet. For wood ashes, double that number but never exceed five pounds per 100 square feet in a given year; so wood ashes can seldom be used exclusively as a pH modifier. Rather, they are best used when mixed with lime.

One further note about lime: A lot of sources say you shouldn't apply fertilizer at the same time as lime because the lime will react with the fertilizer and neutralize it. To some extent, this is true. However, lime stays active in the soil for as long as seven years, so the fertilizer will be affected anyway. As long as both are thoroughly incorporated into the soil, don't worry. In addition, these concerns largely pertain to inorganic fertilizers such as ammonium nitrate. When the fertilizers are organic and constituted of such compounds as blood meal or alfalfa meal, the adverse effect of the lime is considerably reduced.

Though excessively alkaline (e.g., a pH higher than 6.5) soils are rare in the United States, they exist in a few places such as the Black Belt prairie region of Alabama or can be accidentally created through excessive liming.

Correcting an excessively alkaline soil can be done using a variety of substances, including elemental sulfur (known as flowers of sulfur), ammonium sulfate, sulfur-coated urea, and ammonium nitrate. These latter methods are seen to be best practices in industrial agriculture, but they are excessively concentrated and can hurt the soil biology, so they aren't recommended for a mini farm aiming at sustainability.

Some authorities also recommend aluminum sulfate, but the levels of aluminum, if the pH ends up changing, can be taken up by the plant and can become toxic to both plants and animals. So I recommend either straight flowers of sulfur (if growing organically) or ammonium sulfate (if you don't mind synthetic fertilizers). In practice, the amount of ammonium sulfate required to lower soil pH a given amount is 6.9 times as much as sulfur, so you'll likely use sulfur for cost reasons.

Sulfur works by combining with water in the soil to create a weak acid. This acid reacts with alkalies in the soil to form water-soluble salts that are leached from the soil and carried away by rains. Because it creates an acid directly, it is easy to overdo sulfur, so it should be measured and added carefully, and thoroughly incorporated into the soil. It takes about two months to reach full effectiveness, but results should start to manifest in as little as two weeks.

Measured pH	Sandy	Sand/Loam	Loam	Clay and Clay/Loam
4	5.5	11	16	22
5	3	5.5	11	16
6	1.25	3	3	5.5
7	None	None	None	None

Pounds of lime required to adjust the pH of 100 square feet of bed space

Ammonium sulfate works by virtue of the ammonium cation combining with atmospheric oxygen to create two nitrite anions (negatively charged ions), two molecules of water, and four hydrogen cations (positively charged ions). These hydrogen cations are the basis for acidity and they will then acidify the soil.

So, how do you measure your pH? You can use a soil testing kit or a pH meter. The cost of pH meters for home use has dropped considerably in recent years, with accurate units selling for as little as $13. Simply follow the directions that come with your individual meter for measuring each bed.

Macronutrients

Macronutrients are generally defined as being nitrogen, potassium, and phosphorus, as these are the elements that are required in greatest quantity by plants. To these, I also add calcium, magnesium, sulfur, carbon, hydrogen, and oxygen. The latter three are supplied by water and the atmosphere so they won't be further considered here except to note that proper aeration of soils allows beneficial bacteria access to oxygen. Furthermore, avoid walking on beds to prevent the soil from being compacted. Raised beds in general, due to being higher than their surroundings, usually don't have a problem with becoming waterlogged, which helps keep water from forcing out the oxygen that these beneficial microorganisms need.

Most soils in the U.S. are acidic and require lime for optimum growing. Adding lime also adds sufficient calcium automatically. Furthermore, those few soils in the U.S. that are alkaline are usually made so by the high natural limestone content of the soil. So, in general, calcium levels should be fine.

The major problem you will see that involves calcium is blossom end rot. Blossom end rot is caused by uneven uptake of calcium, usually due to extreme variations in rainfall. Usually this can be avoided through properly thorough

Measured pH	Sand	Loam	Clay
8.5	4.6	5.7	6.9
8	2.8	3.4	4.6
7.5	1.1	1.8	2.3
7	0.2	0.4	0.7

Pounds of sulfur needed to adjust the pH of 100 square feet of bed space.

watering. There are also some effective commercial preparations on the market that contain a readily absorbed calcium salt called calcium chloride.

In general, if you are using dolomitic lime for at least a portion of your lime needs, your soil will not be deficient in magnesium. However, the soil chemistry of competing cations such as magnesium and potassium is complex, and a plant could end up deficient even though there is sufficient elemental magnesium in the soil. Magnesium can become unavailable if potassium is present in severe excess or if the organic matter that forms the biological colloid that makes magnesium available to the plant is present in insufficient amounts.

A clear symptom of magnesium deficiency is often observable in seedlings that have been held too long in nutrient-poor starting mixes before being transplanted: interveinal chlorosis (the green turns yellowish between the veins) of older/lower leaves, often combined with curling leaf edges that have turned reddish brown or purple. If this symptom manifests, the deficiency can be corrected in the short term by adding Epsom salt (magnesium sulfate) at a rate of eight ounces per 100 square feet. This form of magnesium is easily absorbed by plants.

⊗ Both the Rapitest and LaMotte testing kits will provide pH, nitrogen, phosphorus, and potassium levels as well as recommendations.

However, the deficiency should be addressed in the long term by adding sufficient levels of compost to the soil and by using dolomitic lime.

Sulfur is an important constituent of amino acids—the core building blocks of DNA and life itself. As such, the primary source of sulfur in the soil is organic matter. Soils rich in organic matter through composting hold onto sulfur so it can't be leached out, and convert it to the sulfate form needed by plants a little at a time as needed. However, even the most meticulous composting won't replenish all the sulfur lost because what we eat is seldom composted. So sulfur, in some form, should be added annually.

Elemental sulfur is not a good choice for this task unless it is already being used to alter the pH of the soil. In its elemental form, particularly in soils that aren't rich in organic matter, it isn't available to plants as a nutrient. Sulfur is best added in the form of either garden gypsum (calcium sulfate) or Epsom salt (magnesium sulfate). It can be added at the rate of five ounces per 100 square feet every year for either product.

Phosphorus is a constituent of the enzymes essential for energy production within cells. The primary source of phosphorus in soil is from plant and animal waste, in which it exists in an organic form not immediately accessible to plants. The phosphorus is converted as needed to an inorganic phosphate form that is usable by plants via microorganisms in the soil. This is, overall, the best method of maintaining soil levels of phosphorus because most of the phosphorus is held in reserve until needed and can't be leached out of the soil by rain.

The process of microorganisms converting phosphorus into a usable form is temperature dependent, and it is not at all unusual for spring transplants to suffer from deficiency because of this, even though there is adequate phosphorus in the soil. This is a condition that is better prevented than corrected and can be done by simply using a good liquid fish fertilizer at the time of transplant and every week thereafter until soil temperatures are consistently above 55 degrees.

You should also test your beds for phosphorus. Numerous test kits are available, and they all work fine when used according to the directions in the kit. If your soil is deficient, you should add phosphorus in the form of bonemeal in preference to rock phosphate. Bonemeal is broken down slowly in the soil, so you should test your soil and add it at least five weeks prior to planting. The amount you'll need to add depends on the results of your soil test; the instructions will be in the testing kit.

The reason why rock phosphate should be avoided is because it is high in radioactive substances that can be taken up by plants. In fact, one of the primary dangers of smoking is the radioactivity of the smoke, which is a result of tobacco being fertilized with rock phosphate. Tobacco is part of the same family of plants as peppers, eggplant, tomatoes, potatoes, and many other garden edibles. So if you don't want to be eating radioactive substances, rock phosphate is best avoided.

Potassium is abundant in most soils, though usually in forms not readily available to plants. These unavailable forms are converted by the microbial life in the soil into forms that plants can use as the plants require it. Though potassium is required for life, its deficiency is not as readily noted as other essential nutrients. Plants are smaller and less hardy than they would otherwise be, but this might not be evident unless compared side by side to the same plant grown in nondeficient soil. Therefore, use a test kit to determine if there is any deficiency.

Conscientious composting practices that return crop wastes to the soil are the primary source of potassium in a mini farm. This is, however, inadequate as the potassium removed in crops that are consumed or sold can't be returned in this fashion, so a certain amount of potassium will need to be supplied.

Nearly all plant materials contain usable levels of potassium, so occasionally supplementing your compost supply with an outside supply of compost will help maintain proper levels of potassium. Alfalfa meal, usually used as a source of nitrogen, also contains potassium. Wood ashes, discussed earlier as a way of lowering pH, also contain substantial amounts of potassium along with other trace minerals. Greensand, a mineral originally formed on the ocean floor, is also a source of potassium along with micronutrients. The same applies to kelp, seaweed, and fish meal. Depending on the results of soil testing, these materials can be used in any combination to supply potassium that is removed from the soil by crops.

Nitrogen is a primary constituent of amino acids and the DNA within plant cells. Though we live in an atmosphere that is roughly 78 percent nitrogen, this form of nitrogen is inert and not useful to plants. In nature, the nitrogen is converted into a usable form through a bacterial process known as nitrogen fixation that is usually done by rhizobium bacteria that live in symbiosis with the roots of legumes. This is why cover cropping is so important (as explained in *Mini Farming: Self-Sufficiency on ¼ acre*). A proper cycle of cover cropping and crop rotation can reduce the need and cost of outside sources of nitrogen.

Deficiencies in nitrogen show themselves quickly in the loss of green color, starting with the oldest or lowest leaves on the plant. Because the rate at which nitrogen in the soil can be made available to plants is affected by temperature, this deficiency is most often seen early in the season when soil temperatures are below 60 degrees. There may be enough nitrogen in the soil, but the bacteria can't keep up with the demand of the crops. It is better to prevent this problem than to correct it, and early plantings should be supplemented with a liquid fish fertilizer until well established and soil temperatures are sufficient to support natural nitrogen conversion.

Just as with most other nutrients, composting should be your first source of maintaining soil fertility. But because you can't compost crops that you eat or sell and because nitrogen losses in composting can be as high as 50 percent, you will need to add nitrogen as it is removed by crops. Good crop rotation with legumes and legume cover crops can help as well; sometimes this is enough. But often nitrogen needs to be added, and a soil test can tell you how much you need.

Sources of nitrogen include compost from an outside source, various fish, feather, alfalfa, cottonseed, blood and bonemeals, well-rotted manure from chickens and other animals, etc. I like using diverse sources in order to include as many other micronutrients as possible. Because we keep chickens, the chicken manure added to our compost pile dramatically reduces our overall need for outside sources of nitrogen, but to an extent this comes at the cost of feed for the chickens. In terms of dollar cost, however, this works in our favor as the eggs are more valuable than the feed, so the manure is free.

Micronutrients

A large array of minerals has been identified as being essential for human health, and more are being discovered all the time. So far, the following are known to be needed: potassium, chlorine, sodium, calcium, phosphorus, magnesium, zinc, iron, manganese, copper, iodine, selenium, molybdenum, sulfur, cobalt, nickel, chromium, fluorine, boron, and strontium.

These can only be acquired through the food we eat. We can get them through plants or through animals that have eaten plants. But, ultimately, they have to enter plants through the soil. Thus, deficient soils, even if the plants seem perfectly healthy, ultimately lead to problems with human health.

Because industrial farming doesn't have human health as its goal, farm management practices have led to a long-term decline in the mineral content of foods. A number of studies have shown that in just a 30-year period, the content of vitamins and minerals in foods have declined by anywhere from 6 percent to 81 percent.[1,2]

---

1 Bergner, Paul (1997), *Healing Power of Minerals, Special Nutrients, and Trace Elements* (The Healing Power), ISBN-13: 978-0761510215
2 Marie-Mayer, Anne (1997), "Historical Changes in the Mineral Content of Fruits and Vegetables"

There are a number of elements required by plants that are needed in small quantities, and are thus described as *micronutrients*. Overall, due to overfarming, these micronutrients are deficient in agricultural soils because they were never restored as they were depleted. Only a handful of plant micronutrients are officially recognized: boron, chlorine, copper, iron, manganese, molybdenum, and zinc. That is because severe deficiencies of these elements usually give clear adverse symptoms in plants.

However, as plants are the start of our food chain and humans require far more than just these seven minerals, soil deficiency in any mineral needed for human health should be avoided as its disappearance from plants means we don't get enough in our diet.

Composting to maintain the fertility of the soil and retain these elements is important. To a degree, as described in *Mini Farming*, these elements can also be added in small quantities to your beds. This is easy to do with elements such as calcium or iron that can be easily obtained, but more difficult with fluorine or strontium. And even if these elements are available, you may be missing something we haven't learned about yet.

The easiest way to make sure the soil has all of the trace elements needed is the periodic addition of ocean minerals. Over the ages, rain and erosion have moved a great many minerals that would ordinarily be on land in abundance into the sea. Overfarming without replenishment has exacerbated this problem. Though I am able to go to the seashore and collect kelp from the beach for my own compost, this is seldom practical for most people. What I recommend as a solution for the most robust and nutritionally complete plants possible is the periodic addition of a small quantity of ocean minerals.

In essence, sea water contains, in varying amounts, every known element save those made artificially in nuclear reactors. In 1976, Dr. Maynard Murray published a book titled *Sea Energy Agriculture* in which he highlighted the results of numerous studies he had made from the 1930s through the 1950s on the addition of ocean minerals to agricultural land. Though his book was published some time ago, I have discovered that in growing beds side by side, those treated with sea minerals do, in fact, produce obviously healthier plants.

The big problem with using ocean water directly is obvious: you can't grow plants in salt water because it kills them. In fact, one of the practices of ancient warfare was to sow your enemies' fields with salt so they wouldn't be fertile. Fortunately, only a small quantity is required, and when package directions are followed

⊗ Wood ashes, sea minerals, and borax are sources of micronutrients for your beds.

not only is there no harm, but plants also become more healthy and more resistant to insects and diseases. It is also fortunate that on a mini farm, the amount of sea minerals required is tiny; so even a ten-pound bag of sea minerals from various sources will literally last for years. (I use five pounds annually.) There are a number of companies offering sea minerals such as GroPal, SeaAgri, Sea Minerals from Arkansas and others. The key is that each offering is a bit different, so be sure to scale the package directions appropriately.

The one micronutrient that I don't believe sea minerals provide in sufficient quantity is boron. You'll see boron deficiency in hollow stems for broccoli and hollow or gray centers of potatoes. The amount of boron required is tiny and can be derived from borax. Use extreme caution because borax in higher concentrations is an effective herbicide that will leave your beds sterile for years if it is dumped on them indiscriminately. Sufficient borax can be added with one teaspoon dissolved in one gallon of water and used to lightly sprinkle over a single 4 ft. x 8 ft. bed before a regular watering. Once a year is plenty.

Conclusion

Healthy plants require healthy soil. Use of composting practices will help reduce the need for outside inputs plus provide optimum soil health for suppression of diseases. Raised beds allow for more aerated soil, higher levels of production, and the use of less fertilizer overall. Ideally, the process of amending beds for pH range and nutrient deficiencies will start in the fall or, at a bare minimum, start as soon as the soil can be worked in the spring. Cover cropping and crop rotation fill out the mix to create the most healthy soil possible, thus making whatever crops you grow more productive. I have only given basic information in this chapter, so for more in-depth knowledge of bed construction, double-digging, composting, and soil fertility practices such as biochar, please see *Mini Farming: Self-Sufficiency on ¼ Acre*, in which several chapters are devoted to covering these subjects in depth.

2

Asparagus

No, asparagus is not poisonous! Well, the berries made by the female plant are poisonous, but the rest of the plant isn't. And the compounds that make urine smell . . . different . . . to the 22 percent of the population able to detect it are perfectly safe. In addition, it is a nutritional gold mine, rich in folic acid, B vitamins, antioxidants, minerals, and even vitamins E and C. No wonder it was cultivated by the ancient Greeks, Egyptians, and Romans.

The asparagus in stores is sold by the pound, so sometimes it is sold when old and the stems have turned woody (so it weighs more). In terms of usable portions, it is quite expensive. Organic asparagus, even frozen, sells for $7 per pound at my local supermarket. If there were ever a compelling argument for growing your own asparagus, the price and quality of what can be found at the supermarket should be enough.

Though it takes a few years to get established, asparagus is easy to grow and can be eaten fresh, frozen, dried for use in soups, and even canned using a pickling method so that it will keep for years. Once you have a bed of asparagus started, if you properly care for it, it will last 20 to 30 years.

Selecting the Right Variety

Asparagus is one of the few dioecious species of plants grown in gardens, meaning that a plant is either entirely male or entirely female, rather than combining both male and female attributes within the same flower or plant as is seen with tomatoes. All asparagus variants grow just fine anywhere in the country, so they should be selected based on your own tastes. Popular open-pollinated varieties include Mary Washington, Argenteuil (also known as Precoce D'Argenteuil) and Conover's Colossal. Though there are hybrid male-only varieties available as crowns (i.e., bare-root plants), I'd encourage growing one of the open-pollinated varieties from seed because of the ease of seed-saving so that if anything ever happens to your bed, you can re-create it instead of relying on a company that may have gone out of business.

Starting Asparagus

Asparagus is easy to start from seed. Start it indoors six weeks before the last frost, and plant it outside when you plant out your tomatoes. Because some of the seeds are male and some are female—and only the male plants produce substantive shoots—start twice as many plants as you think you'll need. Transplant them in two rows in your bed, six inches apart. The next year, cull all the female plants but the two strongest, leaving these so that you can produce seeds. Then cull the weakest of the male plants until you have plants every 12 inches to 18 inches in each of the two rows in the bed.

Planting Asparagus

Asparagus can be grown from either seed or bare-root plants known as "crowns." The primary difference is that crowns are an already established plant and will produce useful shoots a year earlier than growing from seed. Whether growing from seed or crowns, you should keep in mind this is a pretty permanent planting, and the bed should be prepared accordingly.

The single most important aspect of an asparagus bed is drainage. Wet feet, that is, waterlogged roots, are the death of asparagus. Raised beds are an important tool in this regard, but make sure the raised bed isn't located in an area of the yard that gets flooded. The second most important consideration is soil pH; asparagus prefers a soil as close to neutral as possible. Thus, because of the long time frames needed for lime to work, an asparagus bed should be prepared and pH correctives added in the fall prior to the transplanting of crowns or seedlings in the spring. The third most important consideration is light; asparagus needs at least six hours of direct sunlight daily. Fourth, beds should be 4 feet wide and 1½ feet long for each plant; so when growing six plants, you'll need a bed 4 ft. wide and 8 ft. long. (Make sure the long side faces south for the greatest sun.)

Finally, the bed should have plenty of reserve fertility. This is accomplished by double-digging as described in *Mini Farming*, incorporating properly aged compost into the bottom of the trenches, working even more compost—a good four inches to six inches—into the top of the bed. This can all be done in advance. Then, a month or so before planting, add trace minerals and then use organic sources to correct any deficiencies in major nutrients. The use of organic sources is especially important with asparagus because you can't just till more stuff into the bed later (remember: asparagus takes three years to produce, and the plants last as long as 20 years). Anything added later will just be mixed with compost as a top dressing. The annual spring top dressing should be five cubic feet of compost per 4 ft. x 8 ft. bed. You should mix 3 lbs of wood ash, 1 lb of lime, 2 lbs of bonemeal, 2 lbs of alfalfa meal, and 1lb of blood meal into the compost before application, and then cover with a two-inch matting of clean straw.

There is one other very important thing you need to know about asparagus: it loves arsenic, sucking it up like a vacuum cleaner, and it will give it to you. Arsenic is not a problem unless your bed is in an old apple orchard that was treated with arsenic as an insecticide, but the one thing you absolutely must avoid is pressure-treated wood that has been treated with arsenic compounds anywhere near your bed. All you have to do to keep your asparagus safe is keep pressure-treated wood away, and don't try to grow it where arsenic was used heavily in the past. This is absolutely no joke—it is entirely possible for someone who disregards this advice to munch an asparagus stalk and then quite literally flop over dead.

Weeds

Because an asparagus planting is long term, weed problems can accumulate and quickly overwhelm the plants. Furthermore, because the crowns that produce the shoots tend to grow upward, weed control via hoe can inadvertently

» Asparagus growing through the straw mulch used to suppress weeds.

damage them. The standard protocol for dealing with weeds in asparagus beds is to use flame weeding, mulching, or other (nonherbicidal) means to keep weeds away from the bed. Grasses are especially invasive, so don't let any get close enough for the seeds to fall into the bed. Apply two inches to four inches of compost yearly to the bed, and cover that with two inches of clean straw to smother weeds. Pull any weeds by hand that still manage to grow before they produce seeds.

Diseases

Asparagus is vulnerable to a number of root-rot diseases, but these are highly unlikely to manifest in an asparagus bed situated as described earlier. It can also be affected by botrytis mold spread from grasses, but proper weed control as earlier described will prevent this. There are also some viral diseases that can kill off asparagus. These are believed to be spread by aphids, but are extremely rare in homegrown beds as opposed to commercial situations where acres upon acres of asparagus are grown. All you have to do is create a well-drained raised bed, control weeds and control aphids when/if they appear, and you'll have no disease problems.

Pests

Asparagus aphids are rarely an issue because a wide array of natural predators such as ladybugs keep them in check. If you find a large population of aphids (they will hide under the bracts of the leaves), they can be effectively controlled with two applications of insecticidal soap a week apart.

Asparagus beetles are more of a threat. These are usually metallic blue or black and a quarter of an inch long, though some orange species exist. The adult asparagus beetle does little direct damage; it is the offspring that are a problem. The eggs, appearing like black specks, hatch into green to gray wormlike larvae as long as one half inch that eat voraciously. The defoliation weakens the plants.

Primary control of asparagus beetles is to cut down all asparagus foliage at the end of the season when it has turned yellow/brown and add it to the compost pile. This denies the beetles a place for offspring to overwinter. During the season, just vigorously shaking the foliage will dislodge the larvae, and because they will be unable to climb back up the stalk, they will dehydrate and die in the soil.

Harvest

If grown from transplanted seedlings, allow asparagus to grow without harvesting anything for two years. This will allow the foliage to store energy in the crowns that will enhance their ability to survive over the winter. If grown from transplanted crowns, allow them to grow without harvest for the first year. Then, the first year you harvest, only harvest the stalks that appear for one week. Over the next 20 or 30 years, you can harvest stalks for a full six weeks as they appear in spring. Then let the rest of the stalks grow out into full plants to replenish the crowns.

Harvesting asparagus isn't all at once. You'll see a stalk here and a stalk there. The stalks should be cut with a sharp nonserrated knife just below ground level when they are no more than eight inches tall. (Much bigger and they get woody.) Put an inch of water in the bottom of a wide-mouth canning jar, and put the stalks in the water in your refrigerator until you have enough of them to cook or preserve. They'll keep just fine for a couple of weeks this way.

Seed Saving

Collect the ripe red berries from the female plants, bring them inside, and let them dry out on a paper plate. Next, crush the berries and winnow out the seeds. Keep the berries out of reach of children as the attractive red berries are poisonous, and eating as few as seven of them might send someone to the hospital.

Preservation and Preparation

Asparagus can be kept fresh in the refrigerator for a couple of weeks if the bottom ends are in water, or it can be blanched and then dehydrated or frozen. Pickling works extremely well with asparagus. Even though it is technically feasible, I don't recommend pressure canning because the resultant mush is vile, in my opinion. For fresh eating, asparagus can be eaten raw, steamed, or stir-fried with excellent results. Frozen packages can be cooked in the package in the microwave if vented to prevent explosions.

Pickled Asparagus

Ingredients:

60 asparagus spears
½ cup coarse salt
1 gallon cold water
3 1/3 cups distilled white vinegar
1 1/3 cups sugar
2 tsp coarse salt
2 tsp mustard seed
1 tbsp dill seed
1 yellow onion, sliced into rings
4 cloves garlic

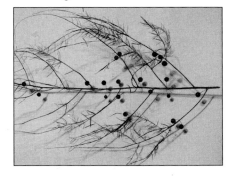

Save asparagus spears upright in water in the refrigerator until ready for use.

Procedure:

1. Clean the asparagus, cut off the bottom 1 inch, and then cut the spears 3½ inches long so they will fit upright in the canning jars while leaving 1 inch to the top. Put the cut spears in a large bowl, add ½ cup coarse canning salt (sea salt is fine, too), and then cover with water for two hours. After the two hours, drain and then rinse the asparagus, and pat it dry.
2. Clean and sterilize four (4) wide-mouth pint canning jars and lids.
3. Combine the vinegar, sugar, 2 teaspoons salt, dill seed, mustard seed, and onion in a saucepan over medium heat. Bring to a slow boil, then turn down to a simmer.
4. Pack the asparagus spears upright and tightly in the jars. Add a clove of garlic to each jar, then pour in the pickling liquid to within ¼ inch of the rim.
5. Adjust the two-piece lids and process in a boiling water canner for 10 minutes.

These can be enjoyed fresh from the jar, as a garnish, or as a tasty addition to salads.

Asparagus berries are easy to collect for seed-saving, but don't let children have them.

Butter Lemon Asparagus

Ingredients:

20 fresh asparagus spears
1 lemon
1½ tbsp butter
2 cloves garlic

Procedure:

1. Wash and dry asparagus spears, cutting off the bottom 1 inch. Cut the lemon in half, setting aside one half for later. Mince the garlic cloves. Preheat the butter in the pan over low-medium heat.
2. Add the garlic to the butter and stir-fry until slightly browned.
3. Add the asparagus, and stir-fry until tender.
4. Squeeze the juice from half of the lemon over the asparagus in the pan.
5. Cut the remaining half lemon into thin slices.
6. Serve the asparagus with the lemon slices as garnish.
   Delicious!

« Asparagus fresh from the garden makes this simple dish a culinary delight!

3

Beans

Beans are one of the most versatile vegetables grown in the garden. They can be used to replenish nitrogen in the soil, eaten as green beans, and made into everything from soups and stews to tofu. They are also one of the most evocative in terms of cultural imagery, with the cowboy carrying his supply of dried beans on a lonely trek and even little odes having been composed in honor of the . . . music . . . we often make after eating them.

The variety of beans available crosses species and is truly amazing, with literally hundreds of varieties available from traditional cultures and more modern breeding. There are seed companies that offer over a hundred varieties! But despite this diversity made possible by dedicated seed savers, the reality is that most beans available in the supermarket are from only a handful of varieties, and fully 85 percent of the soy crop in this country has been subject to artificial genetic modification to convey traits such as herbicide resistance.

Furthermore, beans are commonly overcropped and, adding insult to injury, supplies of dried beans are sometimes several years old. Unless you know a farmer and can get them fresh, the best way to have decent beans is to grow them yourself. Luckily, they are among the easiest to grow of all garden crops.

Variety Selection

Beans can be divided into categories in various ways, but for most mini farmers they can be categorized in terms of growing habit (bush beans vs. pole beans) or culinary use (green beans vs. dry beans). But they can also be divided even further to include lima beans, cow peas (aka "black-eyed peas"), yard-long beans, and more. As they grow well anywhere in the country, the biggest concern is the farmer's personal taste.

When beans are grown fresh and compared, you soon discover a tremendous difference in flavors and textures that is not evident in supermarket fare. A green bean is definitely not just a green bean. There is a big difference in flavor between the Blue Lake and Old Homestead varieties. You may even find that, like in my family, different family members prefer the taste of different varieties. What I encourage you to do is grow more than one variety each year, and keep trying out new varieties while continuing to grow favorites you've discovered along the way. A mix of green and dried varieties is best for menu diversity throughout the year.

Rather than tell you exactly what to grow, instead I'll list some of the varieties that I've grown and enjoyed in each category as a starting point for your own investigation.

Blue Lake, Green Pole: There are many variants of this, some of which offer a wide array of disease resistance. Blue Lake pole beans used to be the dominant bean grown for commercial processing, and it definitely holds up well to canning and freezing. Blue Lake is very mildly flavored and thus ideal for picky eaters who might not otherwise like green beans.

Kentucky Wonder, Green Pole: This is a very productive pole bean that will produce eight-inch long beans as long as you keep it harvested. It seems to never stop! Kentucky Wonder is also very versatile in that, if you allow the beans to mature into a dried bean instead of harvesting while green, they make an excellent dry bean for baking and soups. It is also a good freezing bean with a very distinctive flavor.

Top Crop, Green Bush: If you want to put a lot of beans away, you'll find the production impressive. The plants grow up to two feet tall, and start producing beans about fifty days from planting.

Jacob's Cattle, Dry Bush: This is my favorite dry bean. Not only is it tasty, but it is also productive and grows really well on the outside edges of the corn patch. It is easy to harvest and a very attractive white bean with purple splotches.

Black Turtle, Dry Bush: In my wife's opinion, the best choice for bean soup recipes. It has an assertive but excellent flavor and very good cooking qualities. It isn't as productive as some varieties, but more than makes up for that with its flavor.

Henderson's, Bush Lima: Lima beans are a little tricky in terms of timing the harvest. You want to catch them when they are big but before they start to mature. Henderson's has a very defined "lima bean" flavor with a hint of butter. Shelled out, they steam nicely.

Soil Preparation

Beans don't grow well in acidic soil, so the bed where you plan to grow beans should be corrected to a pH of between 6 and 6.5 well in advance of planting. Enrich the soil with compost, and make especially sure of sufficient potassium and phosphorus. If the soil is a bit low in nitrogen, that's okay as long as you use a bacterial inoculant when planting as the beans will make their own nitrogen.

Planting Beans

Beans can be planted anytime after the last expected frost date for your area by planting the seed one inch deep directly in the soil. If average soil temperatures are under 60 degrees, though, germination will be poor. Though beans can be productive over a period of several weeks, they eventually stop producing, so for a longer harvest you should plant beans in two phases, with the first phase being about a week after the last expected frost date when soil temperatures are above 60 degrees and the second phase being three weeks later. In most of the United States, this is sufficient to give yields until fall. If you live in an area with a growing season of 120 days or longer, you can also plant a third phase in another three weeks.

Beans will generally grow fine with or without any inoculant; however, in order to maximize their utility in a crop rotation based on their ability to fix atmospheric nitrogen into the soil, an inoculant should be used. This will also increase yields.

A little bit of inoculant goes a long way. What I do is put the bean seeds I will be planting in a jar, mist them with a bit of water, add a couple of teaspoons of inoculant and gently swish them around until they all have some inoculant on them. Then I plant them about one inch deep.

With bush beans, I plant them five inches apart in all directions. With pole beans, I plant them five inches apart in one row six inches away from the frame on the north side of the bed. Pole beans can grow as much as nine feet tall, which can be pretty inconvenient for harvesting. You can either make your trellis so it slants away from the bed and put a six-foot support on the top of the leaning trellis, or prune the bean vines as they reach the top of a conventional trellis. Either way will work.

Weeds, Pests, and Diseases

Weeds are seldom a problem with bush beans grown in beds because the beans sprout and grow quickly and the leaf cover they provide effectively shades out weed competition. All you need to do is keep any grass growing around the bed trimmed, and make sure the bed is prepared and weed-free prior to planting.

The two major pests you'll likely see in beans are bean beetles and Japanese beetles. Japanese beetles start as grubs in your lawn (or that of your neighbor's). If you have a lot of property so there is a good buffer with your neighbors, treating your entire lawn and beds with milky spore disease can be a good preventative after the disease has become established in a couple of years. Japanese beetle traps are pretty controversial as a pest control measure because some studies show that they attract more beetles than they trap and will likely bring in beetles from the neighbors. They work well for me, though, when placed downwind of the garden at least 100 feet away.

Japanese beetles attract each other. So one way to keep them controlled is to simply pick them off by hand into a small bucket of soapy water. (The soap lowers the surface tension of the water so the beetles sink and drown rather than float on top where they will climb up the sides of the bucket and fly back onto your beans.) If you keep them picked off daily once they are noticed, you'll likely prevent the problem altogether. They can also be controlled by organic sprays such as pyrethrin and rotenone used according to package directions, but this is a last resort as such sprays are expensive.

Adult bean beetles overwinter in the debris from the prior year's bean crop. So cleaning out your bed at the end of the season and composting the plants is an

⊗ The dense foliage of closely spaced beans shades out weeds.

important preventative. Bean beetles look like slightly larger than average lady-bugs with a bronze cast. They lay masses of yellow eggs on the undersides of the leaves, which hatch into spiny yellow grubs about ¼ inch long. Both the adults and the grubs eat everything but the veins in the leaves of the bean plants, and they eat voraciously. Except in the cases of large-scale monocropping, bean beetles can be controlled by cleaning up the prior year's plants, smashing any egg masses or grubs found under the leaves, and flicking the adults into a bucket of soapy water. In the extremely rare cases where they can't be controlled by these measures, the grubs can be controlled with insecticidal soap or light horticultural oil (be sure to get under the leaves) and the adults can be controlled with neem oil preparations. The most effective control I have found for potato beetles is an organic bacterial poison called spinosad, used according to label directions.

Disease is seldom a problem with beans in a properly managed mini farm environment because crop rotation and debris removal control most likely dis-eases. If you have a problem with sclerotina (which looks like a white mold), switching to pole beans will likely solve the problem.

Harvest

Dry beans need to stay on the bush or vine until they are tan/brown, dry, and brittle. Once they have reached that stage, pick them into a bag, then break open the pods and allow the beans to settle to the bottom. Discard the large debris and pour the beans into a large bowl. You'll notice a lot of smaller debris, but this is easily discarded through a process known as winnowing.

It takes a bit of practice to get the hang of winnowing, but the idea is simple. The beans are heavier than the debris, so if the beans mixed with debris are poured into another bowl from a height while the wind (either natural or artificial via a fan) is blowing, the debris will be blown away and the debris-free beans will be alone in the second bowl. I have found this works best using a fan on medium speed a couple of feet away and pouring from a distance no greater than three feet. Using this method, you only have to pour from one bowl into the other a couple of times to have perfectly clean beans.

Once the dry beans have been winnowed, set them aside in an uncovered bowl for a few weeks for the moisture to dissipate, giving them a stir with your hand once in a while. Then store them in an airtight container in a cool, dark place.

Green or "snap" beans are best harvested as soon as they are large enough to use. If you keep the plants picked clean and don't allow the beans to start maturing, the plants will keep generating flowers and beans for a few weeks. Incidentally, plants grown like this that are not allowed to set seed fix the most nitrogen into the soil. Harvest the beans in the afternoon when the plants aren't damp to avoid spreading diseases, and store them in a bag in the refrigerator for up to a week until you have enough beans to eat or preserve.

« Black turtle beans in a bowl after winnowing.

Seed Saving

In the case of dry beans, simply using the ones you have stored for food is sufficient if you intend to use them the next year. Otherwise, you'll want to dehydrate them a bit using the techniques described in *Mini Farming*. To save seed from green or snap beans, treat them like dry beans. Allow at least twenty plants to grow to mature their pods into the dry-bean stage (making sure that is the only variety of beans you are growing at the time), and then winnow like dry beans.

Preparation and Preservation

Green beans can be kept in a plastic bag in the refrigerator for up to a week. After that, they can be pickled, canned, or blanched and then frozen or dehydrated. They are best steam-blanched for four minutes, cooled in ice water for another four minutes, and then frozen. But that is simply my own preference, and many people like green beans that have been pickled as dilly beans, preserved via pressure canning, or reconstituted from dried form into stews and casseroles.

Old-Fashioned Green Beans

Ingredients:

> 1 lb fresh green beans with the ends removed and cut into 1-inch pieces
> 1 small onion
> 3 tsp butter
> ¼ cup of water
> ½ tsp salt
> dash of pepper
> 1 chicken bouillon cube (use good stuff, not the bouillon that is mostly MSG or salt)

Procedure:

Cut the onion into slices and sauté in butter until soft. Stir in the beans, then add the water, salt, pepper, and bouillon. Crush the bouillon with a fork or spoon until it is dissolved. Cover and cook until the beans are crisp/tender.

Beets and Chard

4

Beets and chard (also known as Swiss chard) are variations of the same *Beta vulgaris* species commonly descended from a sea beet that grows wild around the Mediterranean. Though beets are grown for their roots and chard for their leafy greens, the greens of both are edible. Beets, beet greens, and chard are an absolute nutritional powerhouse. The roots contain glycine betaine, a compound shown to reduce homocysteine levels in the blood. Homocysteine levels are predictive of coronary artery disease, peripheral vascular diseases, and stroke, so beets are definitely a case where cleaning your plate is a good idea.

In addition to this benefit, beets supply minerals such as manganese, magnesium, and iron, as well as B vitamins such as niacin, pantothenic acid, pyridoxine, and folates. Beet greens and chard are also an excellent source of vitamin K, which plays a role not just in blood clotting, but also in bone formation and limiting damage to brain tissues. They also contain vitamin C, beta carotene, zea-xanthin, lutein, and a host of other important antioxidants.

That's all well and good, but . . . are they tasty? Absolutely! And, even better, they are among the easiest crops to grow on your mini farm.

Variety Selection

Given properly prepared soil, beets and chard can be grown practically anywhere in America that plants will grow. I've never tried a variety of either that wasn't delicious, though you'll find over time that certain varieties may grow a little better or taste a little better in your specific location. I'll give you a list of my favorite varieties, and I think you'll find them well suited, but please don't limit yourself to just my suggestions.

Beets: Bull's Blood, Early Wonder, Cylindra, Detroit Dark Red

Chard: Ruby Red, Rainbow (aka five-color silverbeet), Fordhook Giant

Soil Preparation

Beets and chard grow best in deeply dug, rock-free soils rich in organic matter that have a pH between 6.5 and 7.5. The beds should be fertilized normally, though adding ¼ teaspoon of borax (mixed with something like bonemeal or wood ashes for even distribution) per 32 square foot bed is a good idea because beets are sensitive to boron deficiency. One major problem with germination of beets and chard is that soil can crust over the seeds, leading to plants being trapped underneath the crust. This will cause uneven stands with different rates of maturity. To solve this problem, make sure there is plenty of well-finished compost in the soil.

Starting and Planting

Beets and chard can be grown as both spring and fall crops. During the heat of the summer when temperatures climb above 80 degrees and stay there, they'll become bitter and tough. Chard can be harvested at practically any stage, but beets aren't usually ready for harvest before fifty to sixty days. On the other hand, chard and beets don't germinate well at soil temperatures below 50 degrees. In my area, the best time to plant is a month before last frost. This is late enough that the soil is sufficiently warm, but early enough that the beets are at harvesting size before the summer heat makes them tough.

Beets and chard can be succession planted, but in my experience this works best in the fall because the cooler weather during the later development of the beets keeps them sweeter, whereas a second spring crop of beets can be hit or miss depending upon the summer weather. For fall planting, plant your first crop about seven weeks before first frost and your second crop about four weeks before first frost.

It is entirely possible to transplant beets and chard that are grown inside first as seedlings. Though this is seldom done on a commercial scale because of the care required to avoid damaging the taproot and because of the tightness of the timing, on the scale of a mini farm transplanting can improve production by allowing the grouping of more uniformly sized seedlings, thereby preventing plants that sprouted earlier from shading out those that sprout later. Simply start the seeds inside in soil blocks two weeks before the seeds would usually be sown outside.

Whether using seeds or transplants, space your planting at three inches in all directions for beets and four inches in all directions for chard. During the spring planting, plant them about ½ inch deep and keep the planted area evenly moist until germination. If a crust forms, use a standard kitchen fork to lightly break up the crust no more than 1/8 inch deep. Because the seeds often contain seeds for multiple plants, about a week after germination you'll want to go back and thin out the extras. Save the thinned plants—roots and all—for a delicious salad green.

Weeds, Pests, and Diseases

Because the plants are spaced so closely together, once they start growing they will shade out most weed competition (provided the bed was weed-free at the start). What few weeds remain should be carefully pulled by hand.

Beets and chard seldom have pest or disease issues that are economically important on the scale of a mini farm, though in commercial monocropping with inadequate rotation quite a few pests and diseases are problematic. Cleaning up debris at the end of the prior season, rotating crops between beds, mowing the lawn, and keeping grasses and weeds out of the beds are usually sufficient measures to avoid problems.

Leaf miners and other beet-specific pests spread from nearby weeds that are botanically related, such as lamb's quarters; the more generalized pests, such as leafhoppers and carrion beetles, migrate from tall grasses nearby. The diseases either accumulate in the soil from growing a crop in the same place year after year or are transmitted by pests. So 95 percent of the time, just doing basic mini farm

maintenance will prevent any problems. Those few that remain, if they become economically threatening, can be controlled with organic sprays such as neem or pyrethrin/rotenone used according to label directions.

Harvest

Chard and beet greens can be harvested as soon as they appear but should be allowed to grow to at least a couple of inches before picking. Don't harvest more than a couple of leaves from beets intended to produce roots, as doing so would reduce the yield. With chard, harvest the outside leaves first as they get large enough and then the next layer of leaves will continue to grow. Keep harvesting like that in succession and the chard will produce for three weeks or more. As the beet greens or chard are harvested, you can store them in a plastic bag in the refrigerator for up to a week until you have enough to prepare or preserve.

Though it varies somewhat with the variety of beet, in general, beets should be harvested when they are no larger than two inches in diameter. If you wait longer than that to harvest (and especially if you wait until the heat of summer is intense), they tend to get woody. When harvest time comes, grab the leaf stalks just above the root and pull the beets out of the ground. Cut off the leaf stalks two inches above the root and set aside the leaves for eating, and then hose all the dirt off the beets outside. Let them dry for a bit, and then prepare or preserve as desired.

Seed Saving

Beets and chard are biennials, meaning they produce seed in their second year of growth. (Some varieties of chard will produce seed in their first year.) South of Maryland, you can mulch the plants with six inches of straw at the end of the season and they'll produce seed in the second year. North of Maryland, you'll need to cut off the tops, store the roots indoors overwinter and then put the roots out again in the spring. They will produce a flower stalk four feet long.

Beet pollen is very mobile, so if you are saving seed, make sure you have only one variety of beet or chard in flower in your garden. Beets and chard are also subject to inbreeding depression, so you should have at least twenty plants in the flowering and seed-setting population.

To harvest the seeds, cut the stalk when most of the seedpods have turned brown and hang inside upside down for two or three weeks. Then, use your hands to strip the pods from the stalk into a bag, break up the pods so the seeds fall to the bottom of the bag, and discard the larger debris. You can separate the seeds from the smaller debris using the winnowing method described in the chapter on beans. Then, dry the seeds using a desiccant such as dried silica gel for a couple of weeks, and store in an airtight container in a cool, dark place.

Preparation and Preservation

Beet greens and chard can be stored in a plastic grocery bag in the refrigerator for up to a week prior to fresh use or preservation. Both beet greens and Swiss chard contain oxalic acid. Though the oxalic acid is not present in sufficient quantities to be problematic for most people, if anyone in your family is prone to kidney stones, you can prepare the beets and chard in such a way as to reduce the amount of oxalic acid. Cook the greens by boiling them in a couple of inches of water until wilted, and then discard the water and eat the greens.

Greens are best preserved by blanching for 2½ to 3 minutes, cooling in ice water for four minutes, drying, and then vacuum sealing for the deep freeze. Unfortunately, they don't stand up well to pressure canning and they don't reconstitute well from dehydrating. Even so, I dehydrate many greens so that I can later reduce them to powder in the food processor and blend that powder into spaghetti sauce and soups for an added nutritional boost.

If not properly prepared, beets literally taste like the soil in which they were grown. The outer layer of the beet, known as the "skin," needs to be removed. Once the skins have been removed, the beets can be sliced,

This beet is the perfect size for harvest. ❯❯

>> New beets can be planted for fall as soon as the spring crop is harvested for maximum productivity.

rinsed lightly, and then used in your recipes. This can be done by peeling the beets with a peeler, or by roasting and/or boiling the whole beets until tender and then slipping the skin off after plunging them into cold water. This latter method is best as it gets the entire layer that absorbed the flavor of the soil. When boiling beets this way, leave about an inch of the stalk at the top and don't remove the root at the bottom. The loose dirt should be removed prior to boiling, by using a high-pressure stream of water from a garden hose outside or by washing them off thoroughly in the kitchen sink and using a vegetable brush if needed.

Beets can be stored whole for as long as three months by cutting off the tops, leaving only one-half inch of stem, and layering the beets in damp sand or peat moss in a container with a tight-fitting lid. The container should be stored in a cool place—preferably just slightly above freezing. Though beets can be frozen, the results aren't impressive. Pressure canning them reduces them to an indistinct mush. The best long-term storage methods for beets are dehydrating and pickling.

Once the skins have been removed from the beets, they can be sliced uniformly, steam blanched for four minutes, and then dehydrated until hard. Beets dehydrated this way will reconstitute just fine for soups and stews.

Pickled Beets

Ingredients:

6–8 lbs beets with the skins removed, sliced uniformly
1 lb onions, skins removed and sliced thinly
1 thinly sliced lemon (rind and all, remove seeds)
4 cups vinegar (either white or cider vinegar, 5% acidity)
2 cups water

2 cups sugar
1½ tsp pickling salt
1 tbsp ground cinnamon
½ tsp ground cloves
1 tsp ground allspice

Procedure:

Cook beets and remove skins. Slice uniformly. Slice the onions and the lemon, and combine with the sliced beets. Prepare a syrup with the remaining ingredients and bring just barely to a boil. Add the sliced beets, onions, and lemon to the syrup, bring to a simmer, and hold at a simmer for 15 minutes. Pack the vegetables into hot sterilized jars and then pour in syrup leaving ¼ inch headspace. Adjust the two-piece caps and process in a boiling water canner for 10 minutes. Yield: 8–10 pints of pickled beets.

❷ Chard and beet greens are easily preserved by freezing.

5

Cabbage, Broccoli, and Cauliflower

Broccoli made the news during the administration of the first President Bush because he said he didn't like it. But since that time, broccoli, cabbage, and cauliflower have made the news dozens of times in a more positive sense, indicating that the elder statesman might want to reexamine his palate and plate. These delectable delicacies have been in the news quite often for their cancer-fighting benefits.

Cabbage, broccoli, cauliflower, and other plants in this family all produce sulforaphane, a potent anti-cancer compound. Along with this, they are rich in fiber, vitamins, minerals, antioxidants, and more. But the primary reasons they are featured in more meals at my house than any other vegetables is they are not only delicious but also easy to preserve in an appetizing state and to incorporate into meal planning.

Variety Selection

Most varieties of cabbage, broccoli, and cauliflower will grow just fine in most parts of the country if grown during the right time of year. However, because they are a cool-season crop that is frost-hardy, they tend to do better in the north. As long as the maturation date is no more than sixty days longer than the growing season (and most mature much more quickly), that variety can be grown in your area.

My favorite varieties of cabbage are Early Jersey Wakefield and Golden Acre. Both are early maturing and form a compact head with excellent sweet flavor. My favorite varieties of broccoli are Atlantic and Waltham 29. Both of these varieties produce a lot of side shoots once the main head is cut and have a classic broccoli taste. I usually plant Atlantic in the spring and Waltham 29 in the fall. I've had best results in my area with the Early Snowball variety of cauliflower. Cauliflower is vulnerable to earwigs, and we have a lot of them! A quick-growing cauliflower gives the best odds of a harvest with minimal insect damage.

The foregoing are simply my current preferences and will necessarily reflect my own tastes as well as climate and soil. These are excellent varieties for starting your exploration, but you shouldn't limit yourself.

Soil Preparation

Soil pH should be adjusted to 6.5, and the soil should be generously amended with compost and as-needed for sufficient levels of all nutrients. Broccoli in par-

ticular is sensitive to boron deficiency, so pay close attention to micronutrient supplementation. The bed should be weed-free prior to planting.

Starting

For spring crops, start cabbage, broccoli, and cauliflower indoors eight weeks before last frost, and plant outside three weeks before last frost.

❮❮ Broccoli produces side shoots after the main head has been cut.

⊗ Insufficient boron causes hollow stalks in broccoli.

Broccoli and cauliflower can be planted out a bit later if desired without harm, but if you delay transplanting the cabbage, it might not produce as large a head as it would otherwise.

For fall crops, the timing of planting is a bit more complicated but easily understood. Mark the date of first fall frost on your calendar, and then mark the date thirty days after. Now, count backwards the number of days to maturity for that variety, count back another ten days to make up for diminishing sunlight, and mark that day on your calendar. That is the day you put your transplants in the ground. Now, count backwards five weeks from that date and mark that date on your calendar. This is the day you start the seedlings inside for your fall planting.

So, given my first fall frost of September 6 and Atlantic broccoli maturing in 62 days, my projected date of harvest is October 6. The transplants should be put into the beds 62 + 10 days beforehand, which is July 26. The seedlings should be started indoors five weeks before that date, on June 21.

This technique, incidentally, is suitable for any frost-hardy crop grown in fall such as kale, kohlrabi, and mustard greens.

Planting

Broccoli, cabbage, and cauliflower get pretty big, but they can nevertheless be spaced closely in the beds. Doing so helps to shade out weed competition. In fact, it is very rare for me to have more than a couple of weeds in a bed of these vegetables. So space the plants every twelve inches to eighteen inches. This will allow you to fit as many as thirty-two plants in a single 4 ft. x 8 ft. bed.

Early in the season, the availability of nitrogen in the soil is not reliable because the soil temperature may be too cool for microorganisms to work. Because cabbage, broccoli, and cauliflower are heavy feeders, you may see signs of nitrogen deficiency almost immediately in the form of older leaves turning yellow. This is easily prevented by watering spring transplants heavily every couple of days with fish fertilizer until they are well established and the danger of frost is past.

Broccoli grows well closely spaced.

Weeds, Pests, and Diseases

As long as the bed was prepared and weed-free prior to planting, with these large-leaved vegetables planted so closely together, most weeds will be shaded and have difficulty growing. While the plants are small, you can remove weeds between them with careful use of a stirrup hoe; once they are larger you can easily hand-pull any weeds encountered.

As with other crops, the best approach to pests and diseases is prevention through crop rotation and proper sanitation. Especially when growing in raised beds that prevent waterlogged roots and have properly adjusted soil pH, most disease problems simply will not occur.

Cabbage, broccoli, and cauliflower are subject to a few likely pests. Chief among them in common are cabbage loopers. These are the small green worm-like larvae of a nondescript moth with mottled gray and brown coloration. The moths lay eggs either singly or in groups of as many as six on the underside of leaves. When the leaves hatch, the green larvae grow quickly as they consume three times their body weight in vegetable matter daily, leaving a slime of fecal matter in their wake. They have a distinctive "looping" style of locomotion.

Since these pests seldom eat the crowns of broccoli or cauliflower and only rarely bore into the heads of cabbage, on the scale of a mini farm, their economic impact is usually small and they can be adequately controlled by handpicking. (I feed mine to the chickens who consider them a rare delicacy.) If, however, infestation becomes a serious risk, they can be controlled with a Bt (*Bacillus thuringiensis*) preparation used according to label directions. Cabbage loopers have a lot of natural enemies, and among them is the nuclear polyhedrosis virus (NPV). If you are observant and you find any whitish cabbage loopers hanging limply from vegetation, they are dying from NPV. If you can collect them in a can, wait a few hours for them to die, and then mash them up into a water-based spray, any cabbage loopers that eat the coated vegetation will die from NPV in about a week.

Cabbage root maggots can be a problem with early plantings, particularly if immature compost has been added to the beds. These are the larvae of a fly that looks similar to an ordinary housefly. The telltale symptom is plants that look wilted even though they are thoroughly watered. The easiest prevention is to plant no more than three weeks before last frost and never use immature compost. Diagnosis is easy: when you pull up a stunted and wilted plant, there will be little white grubs all over the roots. This problem is best prevented by later planting and using only well-matured compost; once you have the problem, I have found that it can be solved if caught early by drenching the roots of affected plants with a mixture of neem and pyrethrin/rotenone. If the root damage from the maggots wasn't too extensive, the plants will reestablish themselves and thrive.

Earwigs can be a real nuisance, especially with cauliflower, but also to a lesser extent with cabbage. Earwigs are harmless to humans (they can inflict a minor but harmless pinch with their abdominal pincers) but are a nasty-looking brown creature about three-quarters inch long with prominent pincers on their abdomen. They hide in the heads of cauliflower or in the leaves of cabbage and do tremendous damage from the inside out that may go undetected until harvest. I have found no organic sprays that are truly effective in dealing with earwigs, though nonorganic carbaryl/Sevin will work. Earwigs can be prevented by surrounding beds with dry gravel, and they can be trapped by placing damp, loosely rolled newspaper near problem areas overnight and disposing of the newspaper in the morning.

Clubroot is a disease of cabbage family crops that has symptoms similar to cabbage root maggot infestation: the plants are wilting in spite of adequate water. This disease cannot thrive at a pH exceeding 6.8, so it can be prevented by mixing a handful of lime into the soil in the hole you make for transplanting.

Other common diseases such as alternaria, black leg, black rot, downy mildew, turnip mosaic virus, and others can be controlled through conscientious composting of plant residues, rotating which beds are planted with cabbage family plants, keeping weeds far away from beds, and not working in the beds during wet weather. If these measures are insufficient, you can pretreat seeds (which may harbor some of these diseases) by immersing them in water at 122 degrees F for five minutes prior to planting, and downy mildew can be treated by spraying with baking soda mixed one tablespoon per gallon of water.

Harvest

There is more art than science in determining when to harvest cabbage. The heads should be harvested when they reach full size for that variety, but before the heads crack. In general, there's no such thing as harvesting too early, so it is better to be safe than sorry.

The harvesting time frame for broccoli is likewise limited. You want the broccoli to reach its full growth, but you don't want the buds to start flowering. (The flowers are, however, perfectly edible.) Cauliflower should be harvested when the curd is still firm and before it becomes grainy-looking. The key here is your observation skills. As the florets and curd get larger, examine them daily for any signs of florets opening or the curd getting grainy. Harvested heads can be kept in the refrigerator in a plastic bag for up to a week until enough have been accumulated for cooking or preservation.

When harvesting cabbage, broccoli, and cauliflower, use a sharp knife and cut at an angle. In the case of both broccoli and cabbage, you will likely get many individual florets growing on the broccoli plant that can be harvested over the next couple of weeks for use in salads, or several mini-cabbages that taste delicious when steamed.

Seed Saving

Cabbage, broccoli, cauliflower, and other plants in the same family such as kale and kohlrabi can all interbreed. As their pollination is via wind and insects,

❯❯ A perfect broccoli crown ready for harvest.

maintaining purity requires that only one variety be allowed to flower for seed production at any given time.

To save seed for broccoli, just don't harvest the heads from twenty or more plants in close proximity. Allow them to flower, and soon they will develop seed-pods. Once the pods have turned tan/brown, strip them from the plant into a bag, break up the pods, remove the larger debris, and then winnow out the smaller debris and dehydrate using silica gel.

Both cabbage and cauliflower are biennial, meaning they produce seed in the second year. In the southern parts of the U.S. where winter temperatures seldom fall below 20 degrees, cabbage and cauliflower can be mulched with hay over the winter and cleaned off in spring. In parts of the country where the temperature stays lower than that in the winter, you'll need to bring in the plants to overwinter in a cool (35 to 40 degrees) and dark place, such as an unheated basement. To do this, dig up twenty plants from the fall crop and store them in damp dirt in five gallon buckets. When spring comes, plant them outside again. To help the cabbages form a flower stalk, use a sharp knife to cut an X in the head. Once cabbage and cauliflower have bolted, they are processed just like broccoli.

The high likelihood of crossbreeding among this species makes it difficult to save seeds from more than one variety in any given year, but the seeds stay viable

⊗ An ambitious honeybee is busy pollinating broccoli flowers.

for five years when properly stored, so if you time your seed saving right, you can stay well supplied with all the seed you need without danger of crossbreeding.

Preparation and Preservation

With the root and outer leaves removed, a head of cabbage will keep in the refrigerator for two weeks if wrapped tightly in plastic wrap. Broccoli and cauliflower will keep for a week in a tied plastic bag until you've accumulated enough for use or preservation. All three freeze just fine when cut into 1½-inch chunks. For freezing, cut into chunks, blanch for four minutes, cool in ice water for four minutes, remove excess water, seal, and freeze.

Cabbage (as well as kale, collard, and turnip greens) can be turned into sauerkraut via lactic acid fermentation; cabbage, broccoli, and cauliflower can be successfully pickled in pint jars using vinegar. Broccoli and cauliflower turn to mush when pressure-canned, but cabbage holds up okay. Pack blanched cabbage pieces into pint jars, cover with hot water leaving one inch of head space, and process for 45 minutes. Cabbage that has been blanched and dehydrated does fine in winter stews, but broccoli and cauliflower don't dehydrate well.

If you discard the stalks of broccoli after cutting off the florets, you should consider using them to make broccoli-slaw instead. To make broccoli-slaw, peel off the outer layer of the stem and then julienne the rest of it. Broccoli-slaw sells in the produce section for as much as $5 for a twelve-ounce bag. I like adding broccoli-slaw to regular salads.

Baked Cauliflower

Ingredients:

1 large head cauliflower cut into 1-inch pieces

¼ cup olive or walnut oil

1 tsp garlic powder

½ tsp salt

¼ tsp ground black pepper

Procedure:

Preheat oven to 450 degrees. Cut up the cauliflower and place in a large bowl. Add the oil and spices, and mix thoroughly until uniformly coated. Put the coated cauliflower in a roasting pan arranged in a single layer. Bake for 20 minutes until crisp on the outside, but fork tender.

Pickled Cabbage

Ingredients:

1 gallon chopped cabbage

2 large onions, diced (optional)

½ cup coarse noniodized salt

4 cups sugar

4 cups vinegar

1½ cups water

2 tbsp mixed pickling spices

1 spice bag

Procedure:

Combine the cabbage and onion in a large bowl, mix together with the coarse salt, cover with plastic wrap, and allow to sit in the refrigerator overnight. In the morning, flood with fresh water to remove the salt, and drain. Combine the sugar, vinegar, and water in a large pot, add the spices to the well-tied spice bag, and bring to a simmer for five minutes. Add the drained cabbage to the pot, stir thoroughly, and bring to a gentle boil for five minutes. Remove and discard the spice bag. Pack into sterilized pint jars, and process in a boiling water bath canner for 10 minutes.

Carrots and Parsnips

6

My mother always told me that carrots were good for my eyes. That's certainly true, as the beta carotene they contain is a precursor for important compounds that assist with vision. But carrots also contain appreciable amounts of vitamin K, vitamin C, folate, potassium, and manganese. Parsnips are a member of the same botanical family, but being white they lack carotenes. Nevertheless, they make up for that lack with added amounts of vitamin E, twice the folate of carrots, and B vitamins. For some reason, parsnips aren't as popular as carrots, but as they are both calorically and nutritionally dense, if you find them appetizing they merit equal growing space to carrots in a self-sufficiency enterprise.

Variety Selection

There are very few varieties of parsnips available, and these include Harris Model, Hollow Crown, All American, and Half Long Guernsey. All are long-season varieties that are planted in the spring and harvested after the first fall frost.

The varieties of carrots available number in the hundreds and encompass an endless array of colors, lengths, widths, and tastes. These range from the tiny Thumbelina carrot that is literally no bigger than your thumb all the way through the multicolored Cosmic Purple carrot. In general, carrots fall into a few broad categories. These include Imperator-type varieties that are long and tapered, Nantes that are cylindrical and high in sugar but don't keep well, Danvers with a high fiber content and good keeping qualities, and Chantenay types that are short and wide and so better-suited for heavy soils. Even though most carrots you'll find in the supermarket are Imperator-type carrots, these are usually among the least tasty varieties. We eat a lot of carrots. The primary varieties that I grow are Saint Valery, Scarlet Nantes, and Danvers Half Long, though I usually plant some purple carrots such as Dragon for variety. The Saint Valery carrots are twelve inches long and as much as three inches in diameter—real monsters. They store well, have a high germination rate for carrots, and therefore tend to be quite productive. Scarlet Nantes carrots are blunt-tipped and about seven inches long. They are reddish, sweet, and almost coreless. They are a great variety for juicing. Danvers Half Long grow well in tough soils, are about seven inches long, and are a favorite at markets.

Soil Preparation

Carrots and parsnips require a soil that is deeply dug, cleared of stones, light, and with a pH of 6.5–7.5, though they will grow at a pH as low as 6.0. They prefer a soil that is rich in phosphorus, potassium, calcium, and micronutrients, but go very easy on the nitrogen. Wood ashes as a form of potassium are well loved by carrots and parsnips. When preparing the bed, use about half the nitrogen-bearing fertilizer that you would for other crops. Also avoid any form of fresh manures, especially animal manure. Carrots and parsnips will taste just like the manure, and your entire crop will be a loss. You should ideally add *fully matured* compost in the fall to beds destined for carrots in the spring because freshly added or immature compost will inhibit germination as well as cause deformities in the shape of the carrots. The deformed carrots are perfectly safe to eat but not marketable. Stones will also cause deformities. Again, this isn't a problem in terms of edibility or flavor, but it will make the carrots less marketable and more difficult to store.

Planting

Carrots and parsnips are among the slowest germinating crops in the garden. This slow rate of germination can be problematic because weeds will likely sprout first, and there is difficulty in maintaining optimum levels of soil moisture long enough for the seeds to sprout. They also don't like being thinned as they are very fragile when young, and should therefore be planted at optimum spacing from the beginning.

These crops should be planted three weeks before last frost or when soil temperatures are above 50 degrees at a four-inch spacing in all directions. Parsnip seeds aren't too difficult to handle, but carrot seeds are small. If you find them difficult to handle, there are several seed companies that sell carrot seeds that have been encapsulated in an innocuous substance that will break down once the seeds have been watered. These encapsulated seeds are the size of a BB and much easier to handle. Alternately, you can have someone with smaller fingers take on the task.

In spring plantings, the seeds should be planted no more than one-quarter inch deep because the lower temperatures will make germination take longer and the fragile seedlings will have too much difficulty breaking through the soil if they are planted more deeply. For late summer plantings, they can be planted more deeply.

Carrots and parsnips take a long time to germinate, but this is very much temperature dependent. At a soil temperature of 42 degrees, they take fifty-one days to germinate. At 50 degrees, they take seventeen days to germinate, but at a soil temperature of 59 degrees, they require only ten days. Only six days are required at 72 degrees, but germination rates at temperatures higher than that decline. Use of a soil thermometer to time your planting can help a great deal with these vegetables.

After the seeds are planted, you should water twice daily using a fine mist until the seedlings are well established. Once they are established, a weekly deep soaking providing the equivalent of an inch of water is sufficient.

The one growing problem you may encounter with carrots is green shoulders. If they grow up out of the ground, the tops of the carrots will turn green and they will become bitter. If you see carrot tops poking up out of the ground at all, hill them with some dirt and it won't be a problem.

Weeds, Pests, and Diseases

Weeds are a real problem with carrots and parsnips because even if the bed is seemingly weed-free at the time of planting, the long period of germination can give weeds a head start. With the seedlings in such a delicate state, weeding at an early point can be too disruptive.

There are many ways to handle this situation. If you time your planting for a soil temperature of 59 degrees, then germination will take only ten days. Another approach often cited in gardening literature is to soak the seed bed and then lay a board over it to seal in the dampness and deprive potential weeds of light. No doubt this works in some cases, especially with sandy soils, but in my case the soil adheres to the board and when the board is lifted, the seedlings

⊗ Wireworms are easily identified but not easily controlled.

come with it. You can also solarize the bed by giving it a good soaking a couple of months before planting and covering it with closely stapled clear plastic until time to plant. This will raise the temperature of the top two inches of the soil high enough that weed seeds will be unable to survive. What I do is go over the bed slowly with a flame weeder just prior to planting and disturb the soil as little as possible while putting in the seeds. This only kills seeds in the top one-quarter inch of soil, but it works well enough and is quickly accomplished. While I am at it, I use the flame weeder to get all the weeds and grasses growing along the edges of the beds.

Though, theoretically, there are a lot of potential pest and disease problems with carrots, on the scale of a mini farm, if you are practicing crop rotation and cleaning up debris at the end of the season, you really only have two pests of concern: wireworms and carrot flies.

Wireworms are the larvae of click beetles and are usually a problem when growing in areas that were previously sod or are abutted by sod. Thus, they are a common problem with mini farms in particular because raised beds are usually located in areas that were previously used for growing grass. Wireworms burrow into many edible root crops including carrots, parsnips, potatoes, and more.

If you surround your bed frames with a mulch that smothers out grasses, such as a thick layer of bark or gravel, that will help diminish populations over time. Turning up the soil in the beds a couple of days prior to planting will encourage birds to eat them. Also, when we turn the soil, we scan it for wireworms and other grubs and feed them to our chickens. You can also bait the wireworms by burying some pieces of cut potato attached to a skewer (for ease in locating) two to four inches under the soil surface. Pull up the skewers twice a week and dispose of the wireworms. If you put the skewers into the beds intended for root crops a week prior to planting and keep them in place until a week after germination, damage from wireworms will be reduced considerably. Figure on one skewer per four square feet of bed space.

Carrot flies are the other likely pest. Carrot flies look like a regular housefly, except they are more streamlined. Often you won't see them. Once attracted by the smell of the foliage of parsley, carrots, celery, parsnips, and related plants, they fly in and lay eggs in the soil at the base of the plant. When the eggs hatch, the grubs burrow into the roots and ruin them. Unfortunately, you won't find problem until you harvest the roots and start cussing.

⊗ Carrots grown in a box with a landscape fabric bottom to outwit wireworms.

An important aspect of preventing carrot flies is to avoid anything that injures or disturbs the foliage. Bruised foliage is a powerful attractant. Luckily, when spaced so closely together, the plants will usually shade out any weeds so the primary cause of bruised foliage—weeding—can be avoided. If you must weed, do so carefully.

Another trick that works surprisingly well is to attach some wooden stakes to the corners of the bed, and wrap a two-foot high section of clear plastic around the bed, stapling it to the stakes and the edges of the bed. Carrot flies seldom fly any higher than eighteen inches from the ground, so the plastic baffles them and they move on to easier pickings.

Finally, carrot flies (and some less common pests such as carrot weevils) don't like wood ashes. If you use wood ashes when you prepare the bed and water the bed every couple of weeks with a mixture of two tablespoons of wood ashes per gallon of water, carrot flies will be deterred.

Harvest

Carrots and parsnips can be harvested at any stage. However, the balance of bitter turpenes and sugars favors the turpenes when harvested early. Parsnips are best left until after the first hard frost, as this sweetens them. Carrots, on the other hand, should be harvested no more than two weeks later than the specified maturity date of that variety, as letting them sit in the ground too long can make them fibrous.

To harvest carrots or parsnips, water thoroughly to make the roots easier to pull, grasp the foliage as close to the root as possible, and pull while giving a slight twist. If the tops break off, you can use a digging fork or hand shovel to dig around the effected roots and lift them out gently. Cut off the tops one-quarter inch above the root and immediately place in the compost pile. Let the roots sit out in the sun for a couple of hours for the dirt to dry, then dust it off with a soft brush. Carrots should be washed immediately prior to use.

Seed Saving

Carrots and parsnips are biennials, meaning they produce seed in their second year. During their first year, they store energy in the root. If allowed to stay in the ground over the winter, they will sprout in the spring, sending up a seed stalk with a beautiful flower called an umbel that is identical to Queen Anne's lace. In fact, Queen Anne's lace is a wild carrot from which our domesticated varieties are derived, and it will interbreed freely with garden carrots.

Because wild carrots are so widely distributed and this family is insect-pollinated, isolation techniques are recommended for saving carrot seed, though they aren't necessary for parsnips. In addition, inbreeding depression can be a problem, so ideally seeds will be saved from a population of at least twenty plants.

Bag the umbels (using a spun polyester material such as what you can buy as a floating row cover) when they have not yet flowered to keep insects from

getting to them. You don't have to bag all of the umbels, just one from each plant that you will be using for seed. Once the umbels have flowered, use a horsehair or camel hair brush to cross-pollinate. The technique is straightforward: every day for two to four weeks once the flowers have formed, remove the bags from as many flowers as you

❰❰ Carrot flowers can be impressively large.

can keep free of insects at one time. Gently rub the brush over the flowers in each umbel, going back and forth so that all flowers of each umbel have been touched. Replace the bags, then remove the bags from another set of umbels and continue until all of the umbels have been processed.

Once the umbels have matured, cut them from the plant and allow them to mature indoors in a cool, dry place for another two weeks. The seeds can be stripped from the umbels by rubbing with your hands, and separated from the chaff by winnowing.

Preparation and Preservation

Carrots and parsnips can be stored whole for a few months in moistened peat moss or clean sand. The tops are cut one-half inch above the root so they don't suck the moisture out of the roots. They can also be blanched for four minutes and then either cooled, dried, and frozen or dehydrated. If dried thoroughly, they can be stored in the refrigerator in a sealed bag for a couple of months.

Carrots and Parsnip Pickles

Ingredients:

1 pound carrots
1 pound parsnips
3½ cups vinegar
1½ cups sugar
2 tsp ground cinnamon
1 tsp ground allspice
1 tsp sea salt or other noniodized salt
½ tsp ground cloves

Procedure:

Quarter the carrots and parsnips lengthwise and cut into spears 3½ inches long. Pack into clean pint jars. Combine the remaining ingredients in a saucepan, and bring to a light boil for five minutes. Pour this into the jars, completely covering the spears and leaving ½ inch headspace. Adjust the two-piece lids and process in a boiling water canner for 15 minutes.

Lemon Dill Carrots

Ingredients:

1 pound of carrots
1 lemon
3 tbsp walnut oil (butter can be substituted)
½ tsp dried dill weed

Procedure:

Preheat oven to 350 degrees. Cut the carrots to uniform thickness, coat thoroughly with walnut oil, then add one quarter of the zest of the lemon and all of its juice (making sure to remove any pits) and uniformly cover with dill weed. Spread in a single layer in a covered (it is important that it be covered!) baking dish. Bake for 30 minutes or until fork tender.

❯ This dish is enhanced with dill fresh from the garden.

7

Corn

Corn is one of the biggest commercial crops in the country, being used to make everything from cornstarch baby powder to ethanol for vehicles. Unfortunately, it is also one of the most genetically modified. Depending upon the state in which it is grown, between 79 percent and 95 percent of all corn grown in the United States is genetically engineered.[1]

There is sufficient debate regarding the safety of such crops that the European Union currently bans importing or growing genetically engineered corn for human use. Whether they are safe or not, I cannot pretend to know with certainty. Much of the data pertaining to its dangers seems rather alarmist, but the data

---

1   USDA Economic Research Service (2010), Adoption of Genetically Engineered Crops in the U.S.: Corn Varieties

pertaining to its safety is from biased sources. Perhaps the strangest development in this debate is the adoption of federal laws that preempt state laws requiring that products containing genetically modified crops be labeled.[2]

Thus, other than the laws that ban the use of genetically modified seeds in USDA organic produce, there is no way to know if what you are eating contains genetically engineered organisms.

As I have mentioned, I find the data pertaining to the safety or harm of genetically engineered corn rather murky. Other than buying expensive organic-labeled products, the only way to assure the corn you eat is free of genetically engineered attributes is to grow it yourself.

Varieties

Corn is a staple of the human diet in many places, and as a result, many variations of corn have been created for different uses. Flour corn can be ground into a fine flour. Flint corn is used to make coarse cornmeal. Dent corn is used in animal feeds and industry. Pop corn is used to make (you guessed it) popcorn. But the type of corn most commonly grown by home gardeners is sweet corn.

Of the many varieties of flint corn available, Floriani Red Flint is one of the most productive open-pollinated varieties available. Grain yield is roughly five pounds per 4 ft. x 8 ft. bed. Blue Hopi is an heirloom variety with a distinctive blue color and fantastic flavor, though it is slightly less productive at four pounds per 4 ft. x 8 ft. bed.

Sweet corn falls into three categories based upon genetics: Normal Sugary (Su), Sugary Enhanced (Se) and Supersweet (Sh2). These genes determine how much sugar is in the kernel and how long the sugar will stay in the kernel before turning to starch. All of the genes that result in sweet corn are recessive traits that spontaneously arose in flint or dent corn. As a result of the recessive quality of these traits, sweet corn should be separated from field corns that may be pollinating at the same time by at least 400 yards. Otherwise, the kernels of the sweet corn won't be sweet.

Su sweet corns are the oldest varieties of sweet corn. Nearly all available open-pollinated varieties of sweet corn have this genetic profile. Examples of popular open-pollinated varieties include Golden Bantam (yellow), Country Gentleman (white), Stowell's Evergreen (white), and Double Standard (bicolor). Common

---

2   Lasker, Eric (2005), Federal Preemption and State Anti-"GM" Food Laws

hybrids with Su genes include Early Sunglow (yellow), Silver Queen (white), and Butter and Sugar (bicolor).

Su sweet corn needs to be kept well away from Sh2 sweet corn but can be grown near Se sweet corn and vice versa. Harvest timing is critical, and it should ideally be processed within thirty minutes of harvest, as the sugar starts turning to starch the second the ear is picked from the stalk. Even so, Su varieties deliver a classic corn taste and hold up well to being blanched and frozen on the cob.

Se sweet corn has even more sugar than Su corn—so much so that it can keep at high quality for two to four days after harvest if refrigerated. Although some projects for producing open-pollinated Se varieties are underway,[3] all commercially available Se varieties are hybrids. Se corn has excellent taste but is comparatively delicate so it doesn't stand up well to processing. It is better for fresh eating. Popular Se varieties include Kandy Korn (yellow), Argent (white), and Precious Gem (bicolor).

Sh2 sweet corn holds its sugar content for as long as ten days after harvest and is thus ideal for truck-shipping and display in supermarkets. In addition, though more ideal for shipping than eating, the kernels are tougher and so stand up better to rough handling. All commercially available Sh2 varieties are hybrids, and they must be separated from Se and Su types to avoid developing starchy kernels. Popular Sh2 varieties include Challenger (yellow), Aspen (white), and Dazzle (bicolor).

Though there are a staggering number of varieties available, for mini farming I recommend sticking to Su and Se varieties because they are more tolerant of planting depth and soil temperature variations. For seed saving, you are limited to open-pollinated varieties that, so far, are entirely Su strains. I recommend Floriani Red Flint or Blue Hopi for cornmeal, and Golden Bantam or Stowell's Evergreen for sweet corn; these are beginner recommendations and through experimentation you'll likely find other varieties that you like.

Soil Preparation

Corn is a seriously hungry plant, requiring plenty of food, light, and water for optimal production. In addition, it is shallow-rooted, a fact that makes proper soil management all the more critical. Corn prefers a pH of 6.0 to 6.5 and lots of organic

---

3   The Organic Farming Research Foundation has funded a project to create two open pollinated, sugary enhanced sweet corn varieties. Joseph's Garden in Paradise, Utah, is undertaking a similar effort.

matter tilled throughout the top six to eight inches of soil. It is a heavy feeder and in agribusiness production is typically treated with high-nitrogen fertilizers three times during the course of the season. However, this is because the artificial fertilizers they use are highly soluble, and they pay little attention to maintaining high enough levels of organic matter in the soil to hold onto those nutrients. A properly prepared bed won't need additional fertilizer to produce great corn.

To prepare a bed for corn, add at least six cubic feet of mature compost per forty-eight square feet of bed and mix it into the top six to eight inches of soil. Adjust the pH to somewhere between 6.0 and 6.5 using lime. Add micronutrients in the form of sea mineral solids at the manufacturer's recommended rate. Amend the soil using organic fertilizers based on a home soil test for nitrogen, phosphorus, and potassium. Finally, to provide additional both slow and fast release nitrogen, add ten pounds of alfalfa meal and two pounds of blood meal per forty-eight-square-foot bed, in addition to what you have already added based upon soil test. The compost will work with the nutrients to hold them in the soil so rain won't wash them out and make them available to the corn as the plant requires. Using this method, I have never needed to add fertilizer during the season.

Starting and Planting

Corn can be temperamental about planting depth, temperature, water levels, and more, especially when dealing with hybrid Sh2 varieties. But even Su varieties can suffer from staggered germination, seeds rotting in the ground before they can sprout, and other woes.

Though this solution certainly won't work on the scale of the agri-giant Monsanto, for a mini farm it works extremely well: instead of planting your seeds in the ground, start them indoors one week before last frost. Then, plant out your corn seedlings at one-foot spacing in all directions one week after last frost. This practice allows you to skip all these problems and have a nice, uniform stand of corn.

If you don't want to do this, then plant your seeds one inch deep spaced twelve inches apart one week after last frost, and water daily until they sprout.

Also, if you follow my practice of planting beans with corn (see *Mini Farming*), wait until a week after the corn seedling have emerged before planting the beans. Otherwise, the beans will sprout first and shade out your corn.

Corn is wind-pollinated and strongly outbreeding. Pollination is necessary to produce kernels on the ears. Planting the corn closely spaced is generally sufficient to yield adequate pollination, but just to be sure, once the pollen-bearing tops have grown, I reach in and gently shake a few corn plants every once in a while to distribute the pollen.

Weeds, Pests, and Diseases

In agribusiness production on the scale of hundreds of acres and where harvesting is mechanized, weeds are a serious problem for corn. Mass spraying with herbicides is practiced, and genetically modified corn that is immune to the herbicides is planted. Fortunately, on the scale of a mini farm, weeds can be controlled with little effort. If you clear the bed of weeds before planting, a weekly hand-weeding or use of a stirrup hoe between plants is sufficient.

Though in commercial monocropping there are a lot of pest problems, in a properly run mini farm where crop sanitation and rotation are practiced, there are only a couple of notable pests that are easily controlled. Japanese beetles can defoliate the corn and thus reduce productivity. Japanese beetles are a ubiquitous lawn grub. If you have a lot of property so there is a good buffer with your neighbors, treating your entire lawn and beds with milky spore disease can be a good preventative once the disease has become established in a year or so. Japanese beetle traps (available at hardware stores) can work well, but they must be placed downwind of the garden at least 100 feet away.

Japanese beetles attract each other. So one way to keep them controlled is to simply pick them by hand into a small bucket of soapy water. If you keep them picked off daily once they are noticed, you'll likely prevent the problem altogether. They can also be controlled by sprays such as pyrethrin and rotenone used according to package directions, but this is a last resort as such sprays are expensive.

The other notable pest is corn earworm. This is the larva of a large but rather nondescript moth. Though it will attack nearly anything edible in the garden, including tomatoes, broccoli, and lettuce, it is primarily a risk for corn because the damage it has done is not visible until harvest. Because the moth can't overwinter north of Maryland, it tends to be more consistently damaging in the South, though winds blow it well up into Canada.

The moth lays its speck-sized eggs on corn silk. The hatched eggs produce a tiny worm that crawls down the silk into the ear and burrows its way in. It grows as it eats and by the time it is done, it can be a good three inches long. Often, it will not be immediately detected because its head resembles a kernel of corn and it will have bored through the cob and put its head in place of a corn kernel. It can be a bit unsettling when an ear of boiled corn is chomped, and you pull away with a worm dangling from your mouth! Sometimes the worm simply eats along the outside of the ear. Almost always it eats some of the silk, which prevents kernels from being pollinated and growing.

Damage from corn earworm can be substantially reduced with a critically timed application of Bt (*Bacillus thuringiensis*) mixed with corn oil from the supermarket and using liquid lecithin (available at health food stores) as an emulsifier. Mix one heaping tablespoon of liquid lecithin and three level tablespoons of Bt (in this case, DiPel DF) with one quart of corn oil. Mix thoroughly. Apply 0.5 ml of the mixture to each corn tassel. I use a small syringe (without the needle) that I picked up from a veterinary supply company to measure the amount accurately. Apply it to the corn tassel, and distribute it evenly by hand.

The oil can adversely affect pollination but is extremely effective in controlling earworm damage during the crucial stage. There is a short five- to eight-day window when it can be applied with minimal impact on pollination and still achieve good control. If you observe your corn carefully, that time period starts fifty-seven days after the start of silk growth or thirty-four days after the silk is fully grown.

This sort of observation may not be feasible. But all is not lost! You can also judge when to apply the oil by waiting until the tips of the silk have just barely started to turn brown and wilt. If you peel back the husk from an ear of corn, you'll discover that the silk is only attached to less than the top inch of kernels.

This is the optimal method as it provides greatest control with minimum use of materials. However, it might not be practical. If you are raising a substantial amount of corn, the process can quickly become tedious. If this is the case, you can deal with the problem by using a Bt or spinosad preparation according to label directions and thoroughly spraying the corn once a week using an ordinary garden sprayer starting once the silk has formed. The water-based spray will have no adverse effect on pollination and, as long as you don't skip, adequate control will be maintained.

Though corn is vulnerable to about a dozen diseases of commercial importance in large-scale farming, within the format of a mini farm in which soil fertility is properly maintained, crops are rotated among beds, and crop debris is composted, none of them are likely to be an issue at all. Likewise, many of the diseases that manifest in agribusiness production are the result of damage to the cornstalk or ears from machines. As mini farming methods don't use machines, this won't be a problem. If in spite of good cultural practices you encounter disease problems, switching to a hybrid Su corn for future plantings will likely take care of them.

Though it isn't a pest or disease problem per se, lodging of corn hurts productivity in large-scale production and can certainly be a problem on a mini farm. Lodging is defined as stalk breakage below the corn ear, and it is usually caused by severe winds or weather. Because corn is grown in beds on a mini farm, lodging can be entirely eliminated by using deck screws to screw some four foot uprights to the corners of the bed and running some stout string that is resistant to UV degradation around the bed and through holes drilled near the top of the uprights.

Harvest

Field corns such as dent and flint corn are harvested at their dry stage. Harvest as soon as the green husk fades to tan by holding the cornstalk in one hand, and pulling the ear down with the other while twisting slightly. The ears should be shucked immediately, meaning that the husks and as much silk removed as possible. Then the husked ears should be hung in bunches out of the weather where there is good air circulation for a month or more. Once the kernels are well dried, the kernels can be removed from the cobs by shelling. On a small scale, you can remove the dry kernels from the ears by wearing gloves (so you don't get blisters) and rubbing two ears together and twisting the cob in your hands. Collect the kernels and allow to dry further. On a larger scale, you can use a simple hand sheller or a manually operated mechanical sheller. Mechanical shellers are operated with a hand crank and are pretty fun to use. My cousins and I used to shell corn for my grandfather using a mechanical sheller, and we thought it was a lot of fun. As he had never told us to do it, we never realized it was supposed to be work.

The timing of sweet corn harvest is a bit trickier. If you harvest too early, the kernels are imperfectly formed and there is insufficient sugar. If you harvest too late, sweet corn becomes starchy and hard. To complicate matters, especially with open-pollinated varieties, not all the ears mature at once. This is one reason why hybrids are used in large-scale farming—they allow all of the corn to be harvested in one session. Nevertheless, all of the ears of open-pollinated sweet corn can be harvested within a week of each other.

Corn will mature at a different rate each year, depending on temperature, amount of sunlight, and the amount of water it receives, so the "days to harvest" given in the seed catalog is an approximation. Start checking the ears twenty-one days after silk has appeared. When the silk has turned brown and starts to dry, feel the ears to see if they are firm. If so, gently separate some of the husk midway down the ear and puncture one of the kernels with your thumb. If the juice is clear, the corn isn't ready yet. If the juice is milky, it is time to harvest. If it is creamy, then the corn is overripe. All is not lost with slightly overripe sweet corn because at that stage it is perfect for canning.

To harvest, remove the ears using the same technique as for field corn but leave the husks on. Store at a cool temperature, preferably in a refrigerator, until used to help slow down the conversion of sugar to starch. With Su varieties, use or preserve within a few hours. With Se varieties, you have two to three days. With Sh2 varieties, you have a week.

Seed Saving

Corn is a strongly outbreeding plant, meaning that it is subject to inbreeding depression if a large number of plants aren't used as the breeding pool. In the case of corn, so many plants are needed that it may not even be feasible to save seed at a small scale. You need at least 200 plants, from which you cull any that are clearly inferior or off-type. Because corn is wind-pollinated and readily crosses with all other varieties of corn, if you are trying to maintain pure seed it should be separated from other corn by at least a mile, but preferably more.

The seeds of field corn are harvested as described above in the section on harvesting. In order to save seed from sweet corn, treat it like field corn and allow the ear to reach maturity rather than harvesting at its milk stage. I recommend shelling all of the corn into a large container, mixing it thoroughly so that seeds are

saved from as many unique plants as possible, and taking a random sample of at least a quart from the container as seed. The dried sweet corn that isn't used for seed can also be ground into cornmeal.

Preparation and Preservation

Dried corn should be stored in an airtight container in a cool, dry place. Ideally, that container will be free of oxygen in order to

« When the silk has turned brown and starts to dry, check your sweet corn for ripeness.

prevent pests. There are a lot of ways to do this. One way is to put a metal plate on top of the corn and place an amount of dry ice (solidified carbon dioxide) on the plate. Because carbon dioxide is heavier than air, as it vaporizes it will supplant all of the oxygen in the container. When the dry ice is almost gone, put the lid on the container. Another way is to use an airtight metal container, put a very stable heatproof plate on top of the corn, put an unscented candle on it, light the candle, and close the lid. Though this won't remove all of the oxygen, it will alter the oxygen/carbon dioxide proportions sufficiently to be inimical to animal life. You'll need to relight the candle each time the lid is opened. Flint and dent corn can be ground into truly excellent cornmeal using a hand grinder with proper burrs such as the Corona grain mill.

Sweet corn is ideally prepared within a few hours of harvest to prevent the conversion of sugars to starches. The most popular way to eat sweet corn is corn on the cob. The corn is shucked, and the ears are boiled for twenty minutes or so. I prefer to slather mine with enough butter and salt to make a cardiologist wince, but there are plenty of other toppings. Corn on the cob can also be grilled. Peel back the husk but leave it attached, remove the silk, coat the kernels with plentiful olive oil, put the husk back, and tie it closed with cotton string. Then grill, turning frequently, on a medium-hot grill for fifteen to twenty minutes. If you don't want to bother with the husk, wrap the shucked ears in aluminum foil and use butter instead of oil.

❂ Sweet corn should be shucked and used as soon as possible after harvest.

Sweet corn can be frozen either on or off the cob. Blanch for four minutes, cool for four minutes, dry off the water, and put in freezer bags from which the air has been evacuated. Off the cob, it can also be dehydrated following blanching. Sweet corn holds up to pressure canning pretty well, especially if harvested a couple of days late.

Canned Corn

Ingredients:

2 pounds husked corn on the cob per pint
salt
water

Procedure:

Husk the corn and remove the silk. Use a sharp knife to cut the kernels from the cob. Place the kernels in jars, add (optionally) ½ teaspoon salt per pint or 1 teaspoon per quart, ladle boiling water over the corn in the jars leaving one inch of headspace, and then process in a pressure canner at 10 pounds of pressure for 55 minutes for pints, or 1 hour and 20 minutes for quarts.

Fresh Corn Salsa

Ingredients:

5 ears fresh sweet corn
1 jalapeño pepper
½ pound tomatillos (preferred) or tomatoes
1 red pepper, chopped small with membranes removed
1 small onion, sliced thinly
1 lemon
½ tsp ground coriander
1 tbsp chopped fresh cilantro
water

Procedure:

Husk the corn and cut the kernels from the cobs. Remove membranes and chop the jalapeño pepper finely. Chop up the tomatillos after removing the husks. Add all of the ingredients to a frying pan, squeeze the juice of the lemon into the mixture, add enough water to prevent scorching, and bring to a light boil over medium heat. Stir frequently for 5 minutes, and then remove from heat. Put it in the refrigerator to cool, and then stir in the cilantro before serving. Note: this is a fresh salsa and is not intended for canning as it isn't acidic enough to be canned safely.

8

Cucumbers

Cucumbers are in close competition with tomatoes as the quintessential vegetable announcing the joy of summer. Eaten alone, as part of a salad, or as a pickle, cucumbers lend a distinctively fresh and wholesome flavor to any meal. A member of the gourd family along with gourds, melons, and squash, cucumbers were originally cultivated in India and spread from there to ancient Greece, Rome, and eventually to France where they graced Charlemagne's table.

Cucumbers contain caffeic acid and vitamin C, as well as being a good source of molybdenum, vitamin A, fiber, and folate in the diet. Their silica content is good for the skin, and they have been used as a cosmetic, either sliced or as a paste, for hundreds of years to reduce puffiness in and around the eyes.

Variety Selection

In general, cucumbers are classified as slicers, picklers, or burpless, though at the right stage of development their uses are interchangeable to some degree. Slicers are usually long and straight and are intended for fresh eating. Picklers usually grow no longer than four inches and have been bred specifically for their quality as pickles. Burpless cucumbers are supposed to be more easily digested without burping when eaten fresh, but as I've never had a problem with either slicers or picklers causing burping, I can't say with certainty that burpless cucumbers solve the problem.

When growing in raised beds, space is an issue. Cucumbers are usually a vining crop, though some bush varieties have been introduced. In general, bush varieties aren't very productive. Using raised beds, the best space efficiency is gained by growing vining varieties on a trellis on the northern one foot of a bed and using the rest of the bed for growing a shorter crop such as lettuce or carrots. Trellised cucumbers also tend to grow straighter.

One additional complication in choosing cucumber varieties is bacterial wilt disease, spread by cucumber beetles. There are very few resistant cultivars, but if you run into trouble with this pest and the accompanying disease, your best bet may be to switch to a variety of cucumber that is resistant.

Among slicers, good vining varieties include Muncher, Marketmore 76, Tendergreen Burpless, and Straight Eight. My favorite vining picklers are Homemade Pickles and Boston Pickling Improved. If you have difficulty with cucumber beetles carrying bacterial wilt disease, you might want to consider the hybrid pickler County Fair, which has demonstrated resistance to bacterial wilt disease in controlled studies.

Soil Preparation

Cucumbers like fertile, well-drained soils with lots of organic matter. Add at least five cubic feet of compost per 4 ft. x 8 ft. bed, adjust the pH to between 6 and 7, and amend for NPK as indicated by a soil test. Cucumbers like trace minerals, so make sure these are added as well. Organic fertilizers are well matched to cucumbers as continuous harvest creates long-term needs for fertility. Organic fertilizers buffered with plenty of compost are a recipe for impressive success with cucumbers and also reduce the uneven growth spurts that make cucumbers more vulnerable to disease.

 Pickling and slicing cucumbers ready for a salad.

Starting and Planting

Cucumbers can be grown either from seed or from transplants. I prefer to start the seeds indoors a week before last frost and then plant them out a week after last frost to give them a head start. If you prefer direct seeding, wait until a week after last frost, put the seeds in soil one-half inch to one inch deep and water thoroughly daily until the seedlings emerge.

As mentioned earlier, cucumbers are most productive and most space-efficient when trellised. A six foot trellis is sufficient. Plant cucumbers spaced eight inches to twelve inches apart in a single row along the northern one foot of a bed. As the seedlings grow, train the vines onto the trellis. Once they have a foothold on the trellis, you'll only have to train the occasional errant vine.

Weeds, Pests, and Diseases

Plant cucumbers in a weed-free bed and weed by hand weekly. Once established, cucumbers will outgrow most weed problems, but you want to get the weeds out anyway so they don't set seed and create a problem for future crops.

Cucumbers are vulnerable to three major pests: leaf miners, aphids, and cucumber beetles. They also are vulnerable to squash bugs and squash vine borers, though they aren't a preferred food for those creatures. (For more information on these latter two pests, please see the section on squash.) Leaf miners are the larva of a small yellow and black fly. The eggs are laid on the upper surface of the leaf, and the hatched larvae burrow through the leaf, leaving tracks. When ready, they cut a semicircular hole on the underside of the leaf and drop to the ground to pupate. Usually leaf miners pose little or no economic risk to cucumbers. Crop rotation and cleaning up debris are sufficient to keep them at bay.

Various species of aphids affect nearly every soft plant in existence. They suck out the plant juices and excrete a sticky honeydew that serves as food for ants and fungi. At low levels of infestation, aphids aren't usually an economic threat, but at higher levels they can weaken and stunt plants. Aphids are tiny oval creatures about one-sixteenth of an inch long when full grown. Some have wings and some don't. They can be controlled with insecticidal soap or a light horticultural oil applied to tops and bottoms of leaf surfaces and along the stem.

Cucumber beetles are a serious threat because they carry bacterial wilt disease. They can do serious feeding damage as well, with adults feeding on fruit, flowers, stems, and foliage, and larvae feeding on the roots. But, overall, bacterial wilt disease is the greatest threat because the disease kills the plants outright. Organic control focuses mainly on prevention because botanical insecticides are only moderately effective at best, especially given that all it takes to kill a plant

is a single bite. Because cucumber beetles overwinter away from the garden, feed on a variety of wild plants and trees until cucurbits are available, and can be carried hundreds of miles on high altitude wind currents, crop rotation and composting debris are not as effective in controlling them as in controlling other pests.

Some people grow cucumbers for decades and never encounter a cucumber beetle, while another farmer less than a mile away can suffer serious infestation year after year. You never really know

❰❰ Growing cucumbers on a trellis makes them straighter and saves space.

until you encounter them. If you encounter them, here are some strategies for their management.

Grow resistant varieties. Only two resistant varieties exist as far as I know: County Fair (a pickler) and Saladin (a European greenhouse slicer). Use transplants instead of seeds to get a head start. Use floating row cover (well anchored) to exclude the beetles until the first flowers appear. If you use this strategy, you should thoroughly weed the bed and then flame the soil before transplanting, as opening up the row cover to weed will defeat its purpose. Use aluminum foil or Mylar (you can get this cheap as a so-called "emergency blanket") as a mulch because studies show this sort of mulch can reduce pest levels below the threshold of economic damage.[1]

Once you see cucumber beetles on your vines (they often hide in the flowers), it's too late for any organic sprays to have much of an effect. Plus, those sprays (particularly those containing pyrethrin) would likely be far more toxic to bees, and bees are critical pollinators for cucumbers.

Other than bacterial wilt, the most likely disease you will see in cucumbers is powdery mildew. Powdery mildew is caused by a fungal spoor taking root on (usually) the underside of the leaves. It appears like baby powder and is often accompanied by a yellowing of the upper side of the leaf opposite the fungus colony. As the disease progresses, it can spread to the upper sides of leaves and even (although rarely) to the fruit. Powdery mildew infections, if uncontrolled, will cause the death of the associated leaves and poor quality fruit.

Conditions favoring powdery mildew development are high humidity, shade, and poor air circulation. It overwinters in crop debris, so even though the spoors are widespread, risk of reinfection can be diminished through sanitation. Likewise, the variation and species of powdery mildew fungus is usually specific to a given family of plants, so crop rotation will help. So growing cucumbers on trellises for better air circulation and locating them in full sun, along with crop rotation and sanitation will go a long way toward prevention.

Another thing to consider, because many resistant varieties of cucumber are available, is planting a variety of cucumber that is resistant to powdery mildew. Examples include Marketmore 76 and Tendergreen Burpless, among others.

Once an infection is noted, immediate treatment can eliminate the problem. Because development of fungicide resistance has been observed in many variations of powdery mildew, I recommend a fungicide cocktail approach. The fungicides

---

1   Diver, S. & Hinman, T. (2008), *Cucumber Beetles: Organic and Biorational Integrated Pest Management*

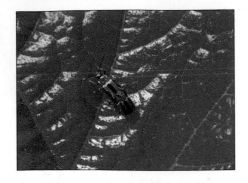

used in organic production, particularly bicarbonate and horticultural oils, have the potential to harm or kill garden plants. So during this treatment regimen, please make sure the plants are well hydrated, and test bicarbonate and horticultural oils on a single leaf first and wait a day to assure no harm is done before making a wider application. Use a pressure sprayer to spray the plants and leaves (making sure to get the undersides of the leaves) with a solution *Bacillus subtilis* (such as Serenade) according to label directions. Wait two days, then spray with light horticultural oil mixed according to label directions, to which you have added one tablespoon baking soda (sodium bicarbonate) per gallon of water. Spray to the point of runoff. Wait three days, and then repeat the cycle. Continue repeating the cycle until no powdery mildew remains, and then spray every other week with the *Bacillus subtilis* preparation.

Harvest

Cucumbers should be harvested when they have reached the size for the particular variety grown and well before they have started to turn from green to yellow. Keep a watchful eye for cucumbers that manage to hide among the leaves while they ripen because once a cucumber on a particular vine starts ripening, that vine will stop producing new fruit. To pick a cucumber with minimal damage to the vine, gently hold the cucumber with one hand while using a pair of scissors in the other hand to cut the stem.

Saving Seed

Cucumber seeds are saved via the wet method. Allow a couple of cucumbers on each vine to grow to maturity—meaning they grow large, yellow, and soft. Leave these on the vines until they are dead from frost, and then bring them in to ripen out of direct sunlight for another couple of weeks. Slice the cucumbers open lengthwise and scoop out the seed mass into a plastic cup. Add some warm

Powdery mildew is preventable and curable. ⟫

water, stir, and allow to sit for five days. At the end of five days there will be mold growing on top. Give it a swirl and the bad seeds will float while the good ones sink. Empty out the water, discard the mold and bad seeds, and rinse the good seeds thoroughly. Dry the good seeds with a paper towel, and then allow them to dry on a screen until they are brittle. You can dehydrate them further using a silica gel desiccant. Store in a sealed container in a cool, dry place away from sunlight.

Preparation and Preservation

Cucumbers keep best at a humidity of 95 percent and a temperature of 45 degrees. In practical terms, this environment doesn't exist in most homes. For short-term storage—five days or less—putting cucumbers in sealed bags in the refrigerator works well. For longer storage (up to two weeks), fully wrap each

⊗ Cucumbers will look like this due to uneven watering. Assuring the equivalent of one inch of rain weekly will prevent this.

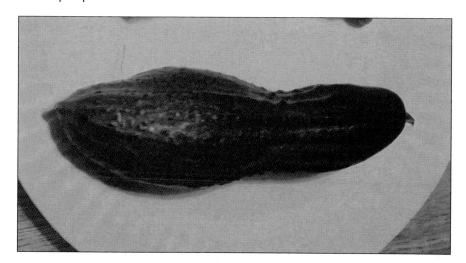

cucumber separately in plastic wrap and store in the refrigerator. That is the effective limit of how long cucumbers can be stored fresh, but they will keep for several years as pickles using any of a number of available recipes. They neither freeze nor dehydrate well, though you can freeze them with moderate success if you bake them first at 350 degrees for 30 minutes.

Sesame Cucumber Salad

Ingredients:

3 slicing cucumbers
1 tsp sesame seeds
1 tbsp sesame oil
1 tsp soy sauce
½ tsp salt
¼ lemon

✪ Sesame cucumber salad is a quick and delicious summer dish.

Procedure:

Peel the cucumbers and cut into chunks. Add salt and stir thoroughly. Squeeze the lemon over the cucumber and mix. Mix the remaining ingredients together, then pour over the cucumber and mix thoroughly. Serve chilled.

9

Greens

The term "greens" includes any plant whose leaves are eaten as food, including cabbage, kale, collard greens, beet greens, chard, spinach, and lettuce. But it also includes a wide array of underappreciated leaf vegetables rich in nutrients that you can seldom—if ever—find in the store. Examples include orache, miner's lettuce, mustard, garden purslane, watercress, garden cress, and corn salad, just to name a few. Greens are eaten both raw and cooked, depending on culinary tastes.

Some of the plants in this category, such as chard, are covered in other chapters. In the case of plants for which I've given more detailed information in another chapter, that more specific information should be preferred. Nevertheless, greens have enough in common in spite of their diversity that a chapter dedicated to their general growth and properties is useful, especially given that having separate chapters on orache and miner's lettuce would be wasteful.

Leafy greens are nutritional powerhouses that combine high nutrient density with compounds that lower the risks for serious diseases such as cancer and atherosclerosis. Some work better raw, and some work better cooked. But in either state, leafy greens, in many cases, literally contain more vitamins than a vitamin tablet from the store. As a mini farmer, you have the ability to eat these greens as fresh as humanly possible, along with growing a diversity of greens unavailable in stores. You'll discover amazing taste sensations.

Growing Greens

By definition, greens are grown for their leafy vegetation. As such, they require a substantial amount of nitrogen. As key dietary sources of everything from trace minerals to omega-3 fatty acids, they should be provided with soil rich in compost and properly managed for trace nutrients. Most greens grow best in cooler weather and are grown from seed. Raised beds are ideal as they allow the soil to be worked earlier in the spring, thereby extending the season while preventing oversaturation with moisture.

With the exception of collards and kale, which should be started from seed in the same manner as cabbage and transplanted at a spacing of at least twelve inches, greens are usually harvested in two stages. First, early in their growth as salad greens that are eaten raw, and later in the season as pot greens that are steamed, boiled, or fried. To accommodate this, greens are usually sowed as closely together as an inch. They are harvested as they grow, leaving an increasing amount of spacing between plants until all that is left are the plants being grown for pot greens.

Often, so-called "mesclun" mixes are sowed. Mesclun mixes contain seeds for a variety of greens that have different tastes and textures. Common mixes contain lettuces, arugula, endive, and chervil, but quite a few also include mustard, chard, spinach, and sorrel. You can buy these premixed or mix your own.

To grow mesclun mixes or use the dual-harvest method described, put narrow furrows in the soil of the bed spaced four inches apart. Sprinkle the seed in the furrows at about a one-inch spacing, and then cover the seeds with soil and water thoroughly each day until they sprout. Start harvesting when plants are four inches tall, and do so in a fashion that will leave increasing spaces between what remains. This way you can harvest baby lettuce and mature lettuce from the same planting, or both small mustard greens for salad and large mustard greens for steaming.

Pests and Diseases

The most troublesome pest of greens, especially milder greens, is the slug. Slugs gobble holes in the vegetation, leaving a slimy trail in their wake. They can be large or small, and seem to be able to work their way through the smallest crevasse. Luckily, there are a number of ways to deter slugs.

Caffeine is deadly to slugs. Spread coffee grounds around plants that the slugs like, and as they crawl across the grounds they will absorb the caffeine through their bellies and die. As a bonus, coffee grounds are a good nitrogen-containing organic fertilizer.

Cornmeal is also deadly to slugs and is an attractant as well. Put a few tablespoons of cornmeal in a jar, and lay that jar on its side near plants requiring protection. The slugs will crawl into the jar, eat the cornmeal, and die.

Beer is an extremely effective lure. You can fill a container 75 percent full of beer, bury it so the lip is at ground level, and provide it with a canopy of some sort to keep out rain and debris. Slugs will crawl in and drown (my wife uses cleaned cat food cans for this trap).

Slugs are physically delicate creatures. Sand, egg shells, and similar substances will cut them severely, causing them to dehydrate and die.

Outside of this, all you need to be concerned about are grasshoppers, leaf hoppers, and similar insects migrating from nearby vegetation. These pests can be avoided by keeping the lawn trimmed near the beds. Diseases are not a problem so long as you practice crop rotation and sanitation.

Purslane

Though purslane is often considered a weed, I grow it every year in my garden. It contains more omega-3 fatty acids than any other land plant[1] and is a rich source of vitamins A and C as well as pigment-based antioxidants. The leaves, stems, and flowers can be eaten raw, steamed, or fried. When harvested in the morning, it has a tangy apple-like taste; when harvested in the afternoon, it has a sweeter and more grass-like taste. If you are eating a diet free of the starches that are used as thickeners, keep in mind that purslane has mucilaginous properties similar to okra that make it a good thickener for soups, stews, and gravies. Blanch

---

1 A. P. Simopoulos, H. A. Norman, J. E. Gillaspy and J. A. Duke. (1992) "Common purslane: a source of omega-3 fatty acids and antioxidants." *Journal of the American College of Nutrition*, Vol 11, Issue 4 374-382

it, dehydrate it, and then turn it into a powder in your blender. Use the powder as a thickener in place of cornstarch or flour.

Sow purslane seeds directly after danger of frost has passed. If you let it go to seed, it will regrow every year in that spot in your garden. The bed where I originally planted purslane has been used to grow greens, corn, carrots, and more, yet purslane now grows there every year with no effort.

Corn Salad

Like purslane, corn salad is often considered a weed; it can be an invasive weed in corn and wheat fields. It is delicately flavored and rich in vitamins E, C, A, B6, B9, and omega-3s. It is best when harvested before the flowers appear and used raw in salads, though it can be good when steamed lightly for about four minutes. It can be sown in late fall for an early spring harvest or in early fall for a late spring harvest. It is an ideal crop to grow late in an unheated hoop house. Germination is slow at ten to fourteen days. Plant thinly—one seed per inch—and use the thinned plants in salads. Leave at a final spacing of four inches and harvest the entire rosette.

⊗ Purslane is delicious, fresh, and makes a good thickener for soups.

Orach

I grow Red Orach every year mainly for the colorful zest it adds to salads. It is best when sowed early in the spring and the young leaves are harvested and eaten like young spinach. Sow seeds every two inches. As they grow, thin out to eight inches between plants and eat the thinnings.

Miner's Lettuce

Miner's lettuce (also known as Claytonia) is native to North America and was called miner's lettuce because it was used extensively by Gold Rush miners as a source of vitamin C to prevent scurvy. It tastes more like spinach than lettuce, and some consider its taste superior to both. It can be eaten either raw or gently steamed. If you have difficulty growing spinach, consider miner's lettuce instead as it grows more easily. Miner's lettuce will grow year-round in a greenhouse, hoop house, or cold frame. Plant directly in the spring at one-half-inch spacing, thinning out to six-inch spacing as the plants grow.

Mustard

Mustard is a culinary delight, and this fact is demonstrated in the dozens of varieties available reflecting every size, shape, and flavor imaginable. Sow in the early spring, harvest the small leaves for salads, and then use the larger leaves for steaming and stir-fries. The pungent character in the fresh leaves is diminished by cooking. The seeds can be harvested as a spice for pickling. A single cup of raw mustard greens has almost double the U.S. RDA of vitamin A and 500 percent of the RDA of vitamin K. It is high in folate and a number of other important vitamins and minerals, too. As a member of the same family as broccoli, it also contains a number of cancer-fighting compounds. And it happens to be delicious, so I grow a lot of it.

Plant the seeds directly in the ground every six inches as early as the ground can be worked in the spring, and then every week thereafter for the next month so you have a continuous harvest until it bolts. Once the mustard bolts, let it go to seed if you plan to use mustard seed in pickle or other recipes. Collect the seedpods by stripping them from the plant when brown, break up the delicate pods, and separate the seeds by winnowing.

Cress

Cress grows both wild and cultivated, both in the form of watercress along stream banks and in the form of dry land cress in fields and gardens. Cress, watercress particularly, has shown a number of anti-cancer properties, including the ability to inhibit the formation of blood supply to tumors. It is tangy and peppery and usually eaten raw, though it can also be steamed or boiled. It is best harvested before it goes to seed. Starting in the spring and every two weeks thereafter until fall, plant the seeds for cress directly, spaced every two inches.

Sorrel

Sorrel is a member of the dock family and contains sufficiently high levels of oxalic acid that it can be poisonous if eaten in large quantities. Thus, its tangy leaves are best eaten young as small additions to salads for variety rather than as a main course potherb when fully grown. Sorrel grows best in light shade but will tolerate full sun. It is a hardy perennial, so if not dug up or killed, it will come back every year from the roots. Directly seed at twelve-inch spacing. These plants spread, so growing them in a raised bed is a good idea.

Arugula

Arugula (also known as rocket) has an assertive, peppery taste. Its young leaves are often used in mesclun mix for salads, and its older leaves as potherbs. Starting in midspring and every three weeks thereafter until summer, sow the seeds two inches apart. Harvest by pulling up the plants and cutting off the roots.

Endive

Endive is a member of the chicory family and has bitter leaves that promote salivation and appetite. It is an excellent source of fiber, vitamins A, C, and K, as well as folate and other vitamins and minerals. Endive can be started indoors for a head start or it can be directly seeded. Space the plants at eight-inch intervals.

Chervil

Chervil is a member of the same family as parsley and has a distinctive yet mild flavor. It is used in mesclun, but also as an herb in French cooking. Chervil is best started indoors four weeks before last frost and transplanted at eight-inch spacing once the danger of frost has passed.

Spinach

Spinach is, for all practical purposes, a superfood. A single cup of cooked spinach contains two-thirds of the RDA of folate, 25 percent of the RDA of calcium, 300+ percent of vitamin A, and over 1,000 percent of the RDA of vitamin K. It is indeed powerful stuff. And for such good medicine, it is also quite tasty harvested young in salads or steamed when older.

Sow spinach six to eight weeks before last frost. I recommend "broadcast" seeding in a bed, such that there is approximately one seed per inch. As the plants start growing, thin to a three-inch spacing while using the thinnings in salad. You can also grow a fall crop by using the same method, starting six weeks before the first expected frost in fall. Spinach will grow up until hard frosts.

Lettuce

Lettuce has a reputation for being nutritionally vapid, but this only applies to the common iceberg lettuce found in stores. When growing your own, you can grow any of dozens of varieties of cos (also known as romaine) lettuce, leaf lettuce, and butter lettuce; all of these pack a greater nutritional punch than standard iceberg lettuce. Two cups of romaine lettuce deliver 58 percent of the RDA of vitamin A, 45 percent of the RDA of vitamin C, and a substantial dose of B vitamins as well. The array of textures, tastes, and colors available in lettuce is unequaled in any other leaf vegetable. My favorite varieties are Parris Island Cos, Buttercrunch, and Lollo Rossa.

Lettuce can be directly seeded or planted out from transplants grown indoors. I do both. I grow the headed varieties, such as romaine, indoors and plant them out about six weeks before last frost so they have time to grow a large head. I sow

⊗ Rich in folate and vitamin K, spinach is a superfood.

the leaf varieties directly, starting eight weeks before last frost and every two weeks thereafter until last frost. I make little furrows six inches apart across the beds, sprinkle seed in the furrows at the rate of one seed per inch, and lightly cover. I harvest the plants for salads until they reach a final spacing of six inches and allow those to grow into full heads.

Greenery Broth (a base for soups)
Ingredients:

> 1 head romaine lettuce, chopped
> 1 small onion, chopped
> 3 sticks celery, chopped
> 2 cups purslane, chopped
> ½ tsp salt (optional)
> 8 cups water

⊗ Leaf lettuces pack a more powerful nutritional punch than iceberg lettuce.

Procedure:

Chop up the ingredients while the salted water is coming to a simmer in a medium pot. Add the ingredients, return to a simmer, cover, and allow to simmer for another hour. Strain out the greens, and reserve the liquid as a soup base. This is surprisingly good!

10

Herbs

A few years ago I ran out of oregano, so I headed down to the supermarket to buy some. Talk about sticker shock! The good stuff in the glass containers was selling for $10 per ounce! That's when I decided that I needed a bed full of herbs.

Herbs are, of course, used in naturopathic medicine. But for my purposes, I use them a lot in cooking to add taste and variety. Being oriented toward self-sufficiency, what I don't want to do is make the guys who own the grocery store rich in the process. I'd rather keep that money in the family budget while simultaneously making sure my herbs are fresh.

It isn't likely that you'll be growing your own nutmeg, cloves, or cinnamon. For those, you'll remain beholden to the supermarket for the foreseeable future because the conditions required to grow them aren't favorable. But other common herbs such as basil, thyme, rosemary, sage, parsley, dill, mint, lovage, and more can be grown easily at home. Some, in fact, are perennials or self-seeding annuals that will become established and return every year with little to no effort required.

Another benefit of growing your own herbs is variety. Down at the store, basil is just basil and thyme is just thyme. It is a standardized commodity product. But when you start looking through seed catalogs, you'll discover dozens of varieties of common herbs, each with subtle (or not so subtle) differences in color, flavor, aroma, and texture. In one catalog I receive, there are two pages dedicated just to different varieties of basil. With this variety available, you can literally grow herbs that cannot be purchased at any price.

In addition, fresh herbs are simply amazingly tasteful and fragrant. Some of the finest dishes I prepare include herbs such as rosemary, thyme, or dill that I have literally taken directly from a bed to the kitchen. The dimensions these add to taste are impossible to describe and have to be experienced to be understood. Dried herbs are good, but not as good as something harvested fresh. Some of the compounds responsible for the tastes and smells of fresh herbs are volatile at low temperatures, and they are lost in the drying process. So even though drying your own herbs is a great thing that will save a lot of money over time, it is the culinary experience of access to fresh herbs that will get you hooked on growing your own.

I grow most of my herbs in one 4 ft. x 8 ft. bed. Most herbs aren't bothered by bugs, so rotation isn't an issue, and those that aren't perennial often self-seed. Some herbs, mints in particular, seem to harbor ambitions for world domination, so pulling up the excess every year as part of bed maintenance is a good idea.

Basil

Basil is an essential herb in Italian cooking, salad dressings, and pesto; it also goes well in broiled or roasted meats and stews. There are many varieties of basil available. For pesto, try Genovese or Napoletano. For a real treat, try one of the red varieties like Red Rubin. As a spice for dressings, try Lemon Basil or Fine Verde. Basil can be directly sown after last frost at four-inch spacing and then thinned to eight-inch spacing, or it can be started indoors three weeks before last frost and then transplanted at eight-inch spacing.

Borage

Borage has cucumber-flavored leaves that go well in salads, and its blue flowers are a nice edible garnish. Sow the seeds directly at four-inch spacing after last frost. Once they have sprouted, thin to eight-inch spacing. Borage's greatest value may lie in its nonculinary benefits. Its flowers are a bee magnet, and it will draw beneficial pollinators to your garden and thereby improve crops as diverse as cucumbers and okra. Inter-planted with tomatoes, it will repel tomato hornworms; some gardeners claim that they improve the flavor of tomatoes. Dried and powdered borage leaves make a very worthwhile addition to meat stews, making them more savory.

Chives

Chives have a mild onion flavor that goes well in everything from omelets to mashed potatoes. Chives are perennial and can either be directly seeded starting three weeks before last frost or started inside six weeks before last frost and transplanted at a final spacing of eight inches. The grass-like leaves are snipped as needed, or they can be dried for convenient use. The purple flowers are edible and make a wonderful garnish for salads.

Cilantro/Coriander

The leaves of this fresh herb are known as "cilantro" and the seeds are known

as "coriander." Cilantro is used in salsas and other spicy dishes, giving them an air of cool freshness to offset the spice; coriander seeds are used in curries and roast poultry. Cilantro is directly seeded starting four weeks before last frost at a spacing of three inches. It becomes bitter when temperatures start averaging over 75 degrees. For culinary use, the seeds should be heated in a dry, hot pan until the scent is notable, then cooled and ground with a mortar and pestle.

◖ Chopped borage leaves go well in salads.

Dill

Dill is obviously used in pickles, but it is also used to spice fish, salad dressings, cooked vegetables, and more. I enjoy chewing on a sprig of dill as I work in the garden. Both the foliage and the seeds can be used. It will reseed itself every year, making for a bountiful supply. I grow Mammoth dill, but other common varieties include Dukat and Bouquet. It can be directly seeded starting a month before last frost, or started indoors two months before last frost and transplanted. Thereafter, it will reseed itself impressively.

Fennel

Fennel has a flavor like anise or black licorice and is popular in Italian cooking; it is also used for flavoring fish, lamb, and pork. The seeds are used as a spice, the leaves and flowers are used in salads, and the bulbs can be cooked as a root vegetable. Fennel reseeds itself so aggressively that it could become invasive; be merciless when culling unwanted volunteers. Directly seed at four-inch spacing.

⊗ Fresh cilantro contributes a sense of freshness to salads and salsas.

Garlic

An entire book can be written about garlic. It is one of the most popular herbs in all forms of cooking, and dozens of varieties are available. Garlic falls into two broad categories: hardneck (also known as "stiffneck") and softneck. This differentiation is based upon whether or not the particular variety of garlic creates a flower stalk. The flower stalk, if allowed to grow, becomes hard, thus giving the garlic a hard neck. The flower stalks, also known as scapes, if cut young, make an excellent stir-fry vegetable. Cutting the scapes also makes the garlic more productive. Softneck garlic has a more flexible neck, and once harvested, those necks can be braided together to hang the garlic.

The best soil conditions for garlic are the same as for onions. Though garlic can be planted in spring, it is less productive. Likewise, even though all cloves of garlic will grow, the larger the clove you plant, the larger the bulb it will produce. So garlic is best planted in the fall around the first frost date for harvest the next year. Plant the cloves with the root side down, two inches deep at six inch intervals in all directions, and then mulch heavily with straw to assist survival through the winter. If you live in a very cold place like Maine or Minnesota, you may need to plant the more winter-hardy hardneck varieties.

When you see the foliage starting to die back, stop watering your garlic. Once the bottom leaves are brown, it is ready to harvest. Don't just try to pull it up by the dead foliage. Instead, loosen the soil by inserting a digging fork six inches away from the garlic and levering up the soil. Then dig out the bulbs. Brush off any dirt, leave the tops attached, and let it cure by drying in a shady, well-ventilated place away from rain. After curing, you can remove the tops and store in the dark in mesh bags. Softneck varieties can keep for as long as eight months, but hardneck varieties will only keep for four months.

All garlic varieties can be successfully pickled in vinegar for long-term storage and can likewise be blanched for four minutes and then frozen or dehydrated. (Once dehydrated, you can make your own garlic powder by putting the dehydrated garlic in a blender.) Though it is a popular practice, I would discourage putting fresh garlic cloves in olive oil for storage, as this provides good conditions for growth of undetectable botulism. In fact, people have died as a result. In 1989 the FDA issued the following statement about fresh garlic in olive oil:

> To be safe . . . garlic-in-oil products should contain additional ingredients—
> specific levels of microbial inhibitors or acidifying agents such as phosphoric

or citric acid. . . . Unrefrigerated garlic-in-oil mixes lacking antimicrobial agents can permit the growth of Clostridium botulinum bacteria with subsequent toxin production without affecting the taste and smell of the products. Toxin production can occur even when a small number of Clostridium botulinum spores are present in the garlic. When the spore-containing garlic is bottled and covered with oil, an oxygen-free environment is created that promotes the germination of spores and the growth of microorganisms at temperatures as low as 50 degrees Fahrenheit.[1]

Lemon Balm

Lemon balm makes a pleasant tea, but is also a welcome addition to mushroom and asparagus dishes, as well as to sauces and marinades for fish and meats. It is a perennial herb that will overwinter throughout most of the continental United States. The seeds won't germinate below 70 degrees and can be started indoors and then transplanted or sprinkled outdoors (but not covered) and then watered frequently until they sprout.

Lovage

Lovage's unique celery-like flavor goes well in all sorts of stews and stuffings while adding new possibilities for salad dressings, herb butters, and fruit dishes. Lovage will grow to be about six feet tall and comes back every year, so you only need one plant. Start a few seeds indoors about six weeks before last frost, and then transplant the best one outside on the north side of your herb bed. Lovage is best used fresh; the dried herb is marginally useful, although blanching and freezing works pretty well. In place of the dried herb, you can use the seeds year-round. They are a bit sweeter than the leaves, but otherwise carry the same excellent flavor.

Marjoram

Marjoram is a close relative of oregano, although it is more mild and sweet, complementing practically any meat dish. Although it is a perennial herb in its native regions, it is somewhat cold-sensitive and won't survive the winters in

---

1   The FDA Memo on Garlic-in-Oil Preparations, 4/17/1989

Like lemon balm, lemon verbena contributes a citrus and savory essence to marinades. ❯❯

the northern parts of the country. All is not lost, however, because it can be successfully grown as an annual by starting the seeds inside six weeks before last frost and putting out the transplants just after the last frost. Transplant at a spacing of twelve inches. The herb is harvested by cutting a section of growth and hanging it upside down in the shade until dry.

Mint

There are many mint varieties available, ranging from the common spearmint, catnip, and peppermint to more exotic mints with flavors such as lemon and chocolate. Mint is best started indoors six weeks before last frost and then planted outside at twelve-inch spacing after last frost. It is a hardy perennial that will come back year after year throughout the continental United States. Its flowers attract bees in abundance, and it can self-seed to the point of becoming invasive if you don't keep an eye on it and ruthlessly cull invaders. In most mint varieties, the greatest concentration of flavor is in the top five to seven inches of growth. Snip that completely—stem and all—near midsummer, hang upside down in a shady but well-ventilated place to dry, and then use the leaves as seasoning, in tea, etc. Mints, in general, can attract cats.

Mustard

Growing mustard and harvesting the seed is covered in the chapter on greens. The seeds are used as a spice, both in whole form when making pickles and ground as an addition to practically anything that can be cooked. It is especially good when used as a flavoring for boiled cabbage, but likely the biggest attraction for purposes of self-sufficiency is the ability to make your own prepared mustard, so I'll include a recipe at the end of this chapter.

Oregano

Oregano is a perennial that is more cold-hardy than its cousin marjoram, and will overwinter well throughout the continental United States. It should be started indoors six weeks before last frost and then transplanted outdoors at a spacing of twelve inches sometime after last frost. Don't cover the seeds because they need light to germinate. Oregano is known as the essential Italian herb, but it goes well with almost everything. I like to add a small amount to portobella mushrooms fried in butter. Oregano is best harvested before the plant flowers. Cut a stalk all the way down to the ground to encourage a bushy habit. You can then hang it upside down to dry in the shade away from weather and then strip the leaves, or strip the leaves from the stem directly for fresh use.

Parsley

Everyone has seen parsley used as a garnish, and many swear by parsley as a remedy for halitosis, but by far my favorite use is as an ingredient in vegetable juices that I make with my juice machine. I use a half pound of carrots, two stalks of celery, and a handful of parsley to make the juice. The parsley makes the juice taste fresh and vibrant. There are two primary types of parsley: flat-leaved and curly-leaved varieties. Though some claim one variety tastes better than the other, I think they are both quite good.

    Parsley is hard to start from seed. To start it, put the seeds in the freezer for a week, then put them in a wet paper towel sealed in a zippered plastic bag overnight before planting inside. They will take nearly a month to germinate. Once they have been established for a couple of weeks, transplant them outside at a spacing of twelve inches. Harvest by cutting entire stems back to the ground to encourage more

❮❮ This chocolate mint makes excellent teas but will take over the beds if you allow it!

growth. It is best eaten fresh, but it can be quickly blanched (one minute) and dehydrated as well.

Rosemary

Rosemary is a perennial herb best known for its use in poultry seasoning, but it is also useful in marinades and vegetables. Though it is supposedly only winter-hardy through zone 6, my rosemary comes back every year in the more chilly zone 5. Rosemary is most easily started as a purchased plant from a nursery or from a cutting taken from an established plant; it is nevertheless possible to start from seed using the same method as described with parsley. The germination rate is very low, so plant five times as much seed as you think you'll need. Put out the transplants at eight-inch spacing two weeks before last frost. Harvest rosemary by cutting healthy branches, tying them together, and hanging them upside down out of the weather until dry.

Sage

The uses of sage overlap those of rosemary; I have found that in marinades for various meats, one spice will be better than the other. Like rosemary, sage is most easily started from a nursery plant or a cutting, but with difficulty it can be started from seed using the same method as with parsley. Space plants at twelve-inch intervals, and don't harvest the first year. In subsequent years, harvest healthy branches that are hung upside down inside to dry. Sage is also excellent in stews when used fresh from the plant.

Tarragon

There are two varieties of tarragon: Russian and French. The French variety (*Artemisia dracunculus*) is more flavorful but seldom produces seeds, and therefore must be started from a cutting or purchased from a nursery. The Russian variety (*Artemisia dracunculoides*) can be started from seed, is more prolific, and has a milder flavor. Both are superb as flavorings for various species of white fish, as well as for making herbal vinegars for salads. Sow Russian tarragon seeds indoors six weeks before last frost, and plant out shortly after last frost. You'll probably only want or need one plant, as it grows to be two feet tall and two feet wide.

The leaves don't smell like much when growing, but once harvested the flavor starts to concentrate. The heat of cooking releases even more flavor, so it is easy to overuse tarragon. Tarragon can be used fresh, it can be dried on a dehydrator, or the sprigs can be sealed in airtight bags and frozen.

Thyme

A classic and essential herb, thyme lends its flavors to dressings, vegetables, and meats alike. Thyme is a perennial, though different varieties have different cold tolerance, so make sure the variety you choose will overwinter in your area. Sow the seeds indoors six weeks before last frost, and then transplant shortly after last frost at eighteen-inch spacing. Early in its life thyme grows slowly, so weed control is important. Also, for its first year, don't harvest from the plants. From the second year and thereafter, harvest around midsummer, just before it blooms or just as it is blooming. Cut off the top four or five inches, and dry it inside in the shade.

How to Make Mustard

The prepared mustard available in the store is made from vinegar, water, mustard seed, salt, turmeric, and other spices such as garlic. Each of these ingredients serves a particular purpose due to the nature of the active ingredients in mustard seed.

Just as the irritant substances in onions and garlic are released by mechanical damage to the cells of the bulbs, the distinctive tastes and smells of mustard seed are released by mechanical damage to the seed. Likewise, applying heat to the damaged mustard seed inactivates the compounds, so the degree of spiciness of mustard can be controlled by the amount of heat applied.

There are three types of mustard seed: the milder white/yellow mustard used in American mustards, the tangier brown prevalent in European mustards, and the fiery black that predominates Asian cuisine. For your first experiments with making mustard, I recommend using mostly yellow and a bit of brown.

For processing, whole mustard seed should be soaked overnight in water. Once it has

❰❰ Sage will reward you abundantly year after year.

This creeping thyme is featured in homemade salad dressings. ❯❯

soaked, process it with the soaking water in a blender. Just as is, the properties of the mustard would dissipate in a few days. Wait ten minutes or so, and then add vinegar and process further in the blender. Salt is also needed to fix the qualities of the mustard, and anywhere from 1 teaspoon to 2 teaspoons is used per cup of product. The turmeric is used for imparting a yellow color. The reason why the famous "Grey Poupon" mustard lacks the distinctive fluorescent yellow color of American mustard is because it lacks turmeric. Turmeric lends a taste all its own, so if you are used to American-style mustards, you'll want to add this ingredient as well. Freshly made mustard is unbearably bitter, but this bitterness will disappear once it has been refrigerated for 24 hours. I have only provided one recipe, but by explaining the process, you can branch out to create your own.

Down-Home Mustard

Ingredients:

1/3 cup water
½ cup wine vinegar
½ cup mustard seed, yellow and brown
2 tsp salt
½ tsp turmeric
½ tsp garlic powder

Procedure:

Soak the seeds in the water overnight at room temperature. Dump them in the blender, and blend until it is smooth enough for your purposes. Add the remaining ingredients, blend thoroughly, and then dump into a sealed container. Store in the refrigerator, and allow to sit at least a day before sampling.

11

Melons

The quintessential taste of summer is the melon. Whether it be watermelon, honeydew, or cantaloupe, melons just seem to concentrate summer's essential sweetness. And even though they are nature's candy, they are very healthful as well. Watermelon contains citrulline, an arginine precursor that relaxes blood vessels and indirectly supports nitric oxide synthesis.[1] It likewise contains a great deal of lycopene, known to help prevent prostate, breast, and lung cancer. Cantaloupe is so tasty that it is hard to believe that a single cup contains more than the RDA of both vitamins A and C.

---

1   Nitric oxide synthesis is necessary for achieving and maintaining erections. Studies show that watermelon can assist in that regard. *Science Daily*, July 1, 2008, "Watermelon May Have Viagra-Effect."

Melons are members of the same family as cucumbers and squash, and there are likely a hundred varieties around the world. Many are eaten fresh, but just as many are pickled as condiments or used to make preserves.

In the United States, we typically think in terms of three melon variations: watermelons, cantaloupes, and honeydew. In reality, the melon with netted skin that we in the United States call a "cantaloupe" is a muskmelon, *Cucumis melo var. reticulatus*. True cantaloupes, *Cucumis melo var. cantalupensis*, have scaled rinds and are much more common in Europe than in the United States. Honeydew, Crenshaw, and casaba melons are *Cucumis melo var. inodorus*. But all variations of *Cucumis melo* can interbreed with each other, so if you are growing them for seed, you will need to practice isolation techniques to keep seed lines pure.

Watermelons are *Citrullus lanatus* and will cross with other watermelons and citron, but not with any other melons grown in the United States.

Variety Selection

Plants that make fruits require sun to make them, so melons in particular tend to be long-season crops, with some requiring more than 100 frost-free days—preferably warm days. Particularly if you live in the northern parts of the country, you should choose a variety that will produce ripe fruit within your growing season with some room to spare.

Another consideration is disease resistance. Watermelons are pretty much resistant to bacterial wilt, but all varieties of muskmelon are susceptible. Powdery mildew and mosaic virus can pose a problem with melons, but resistant cultivars are available.

In New Hampshire, I have successfully grown Moon and Stars and Sugar Baby watermelons, and Hale's Best and Green Machine melon varieties.

Soil Preparation

Like other members of the cucumber family, melons prefer fertile, well-drained soil with lots of organic matter. The use of raised beds assists with drainage. Add at least three cubic feet of compost per 4 ft. x 8 ft. bed, adjust the pH to between 6 and 7, and amend for NPK as indicated by a soil test. Melons use a lot of nitrogen, so make sure to combine nitrogen sources that release both quickly (such as blood meal) and slowly (such as alfalfa meal) when amending the soil.

Starting and Planting

Melons can be grown either from seed or from transplants. I prefer to start the seeds indoors a week before last frost and then plant them out a week after last frost to give them a head start. If you prefer direct seeding, wait until a week after last frost or until the soil temperature is 65 degrees, put the seeds in soil one inch deep, and water thoroughly daily until the seedlings emerge. Space melon plants at one per foot. If planting from seed, plant two seeds every foot and then use scissors to snip off the least strong of the two that sprout.

Melons, theoretically, can be grown in the northern one foot of a bed on a trellis for highest space efficiency—just as cucumbers—and I have successfully done this with muskmelons by supporting the growing melons with a sling made from old washed nylons (a.k.a. pantyhose). It turned out to be labor intensive and would work better with true cantaloupes because those don't slip off the vine. What I recommend instead is planting the melons six to twelve inches back from the south side of the bed, allowing the vines to trail along the yard or the area between beds. I mulch the area covered by vines with grass clippings (or hay can be used) and set board under the growing melons to keep them off the ground. The northern portion of the bed can be planted with other crops.

One thing to consider is planting trellised cucumbers on the north side of a bed, free-running melons on the south side of the bed, and closely spaced bush beans treated with inoculant down the center for a continuous supply of nitrogen.

Melons tend to have shallow root systems. Considering their need for water, it is important to establish the deepest root systems possible. To this end, watering should be done only weekly unless the weather is abominably hot; the watering should be extremely thorough each time it is done. Use a rain gage, and in any week when less than an inch of water was received, give them an inch of water on top of what they already have. If an inch or more of water was received that week, you can let it pass as long as the vines look okay.

Weeds, Pests, and Diseases

Melons are fast growing once they get started and tend to shade out weed competition, so weeds aren't usually a direct problem, but they can be an indirect problem as a reservoir of disease organisms and a hiding place for pests. It is practically impossible to weed efficiently around melon vines without risk of harming the vines, so mulching is the best option. In my own mini farm, I usually use grass clippings because they are abundant, free, and return their elements to the soil. But if you have trouble getting melons to ripen within your season, I recommend killing two birds with one stone by using black weed barrier that suppresses weeds while allowing water and air to penetrate.

Once watermelon plants have grown to have ten leaves or more, they are immune to the bacterial wilt disease transmitted by cucumber beetles. Even so, if present in large numbers they can decrease the vigor of the plant through the mechanical damage of feeding, and their larvae can hurt the roots, causing the vines to wilt and die. Planting nasturtiums around the stems of watermelons can help prevent the adults from laying eggs around the stem and thus prevent root damage, but once adult numbers are noticeable, chemical controls may become necessary. Natural alternatives include using a fine clay product called Surround, or the use of a mixture of pyrethrin, rotenone, and neem.

Muskmelons are not immune to bacterial wilt and, in fact, are almost as susceptible as cucumbers. The most effective natural way of dealing with cucumber beetles spreading bacterial wilt to muskmelons is to seal the melons up tightly under floating row covers until the flowers appear.

Aphids can sometimes spread from surrounding vegetation to melons in sufficient quantities to pose a risk to the plant. If this happens, two applications of insecticidal soap spaced five days apart will usually get rid of them.

Other than bacterial wilt, the next most likely disease to be encountered is powdery mildew. Powdery mildew starts on the underside of the leaf and then spreads. It can become a serious problem if conditions are shady. If you have a problem with bacterial wilt, resistant varieties of melon are available, and you should grow resistant varieties in future seasons.

Once an infection is discovered, fast treatment can eliminate the problem. Because development of fungicide resistance has been observed in many variations of powdery mildew, I recommend a fungicide cocktail approach. The fungicides used in organic production, particularly bicarbonate and horticultural oils, have the potential to harm or kill garden plants. So during this treatment regimen, make sure the plants are well hydrated, and test bicarbonate and horticultural oils on a single leaf first and wait a day to assure no harm is done before making a wider application.

Use a pressure sprayer to spray the plants and leaves, making sure to get the undersides of the leaves, with a solution of *Bacillus subtilis* (such as Serenade) according to label directions. Wait two days, then spray with light horticultural oil mixed according to label directions and to which you have added one tablespoon baking soda (sodium bicarbonate) per gallon of water. Spray to the point of runoff. Wait three days, and then repeat the cycle. Continue repeating the cycle until no powdery mildew remains, and then spray every other week with the *Bacillus subtilis* preparation.

Harvest

Timing the harvest of watermelons is sometimes seen as a black art, where only those initiated to the secrets of the unique sounds melons make when rapped can make such determinations. Most certainly, with watermelons, a very experienced person can do so. But you can also tell by looking for three signs: the curly tendril opposite the stem of the melon has turned brown and/or died, the spot where the watermelon was touching the ground has changed from white to yellow, and the rind of the melon has become a bit less shiny. The stem to the watermelon should be cut with a sharp knife to harvest. It should never just be pulled.

Muskmelons should be harvested when the netting is well defined, they are fragrant, and there is a bit of "give" when the blossom end is pushed. A ripe muskmelon will also slip easily from the vine when pulled. If it is stubborn, it isn't ripe yet—give it another couple of days. Muskmelons are harvested by pulling them from the vines.

Overripe watermelons, incidentally, will explode. When I first started growing watermelons, I had no idea how to tell when they were ripe, so I just let them grow until the vines they were on were dead, and then I brought them in the house. For some reason, I also suffered under the notion that they would keep for a long time sitting out, just like squash. So I brought in some thirty-plus–pound melons, put them on the kitchen table, and let them sit for a couple of weeks. One day when I was in the living room, I heard a "thud" reminiscent of a sledgehammer hitting something. I ran into the kitchen to find a most impressive mess all over the table, chairs, floor, walls, and more. You have been warned!

◄◄ This watermelon shows yellow instead of white where it was touching the ground, and so it is ready for harvest.

Seed Saving

Melons are insect-pollinated, and if pollinated naturally, only one variety should be grown or it should be isolated from other varieties by at least one-quarter mile. The seeds are ready when the melon is ripe to eat, and they are best collected using the wet method. Put the seeds and a bit of the pulp into a large plastic cup, add a cup of water, stir, and allow to sit for three days. At the end of three days, clean off any scum and discard any floating seeds. Then, wash and dry the seeds that remain, and dry them over a desiccant for a week before storing in a dark, cool place in a sealed container (see *Mini Farming* for more information on desiccants).

Preparation and Preservation

Melons don't keep long—maybe a week at room temperature or two weeks in the refrigerator, tops. Preparation consists of just slicing it up and eating it!

You could dehydrate melons, but as they are mostly water, you wouldn't get much after the dehydrating process. Muskmelons can be cubed and frozen with some success, but watermelon won't come out well at all.

The only effective way to make sure excess melons don't go to waste is to turn them into preserves, pickles, sorbets, or even wines. The good news is that even in such states, many of the preserves still retain important nutritional components such as vitamins and antioxidants. That makes me happy because watermelon rind pickles have been my favorite since childhood!

Muskmelon Ice
Ingredients:

> 4 cups cubed muskmelon
> 2 cups water
> ½ cup sugar
> 2 tbsp fresh-squeezed lime juice
> (don't use the bottled kind)
> ¼ tsp vanilla extract
> ⅛ tsp cinnamon

The netting is well defined and it slipped from the vine easily, indicating ripeness. ❯❯

Procedure:

Place all the ingredients in a blender and process until smooth. Pour into clean ice cube trays and allow to freeze. Once frozen, store the cubes in sealed freezer bags. To serve, put the cubes into the blender and break them up, or just put them in a bowl and use the edge of a spoon to eat them a little at a time.

Watermelon Rind Pickles

Ingredients:

4 quarts cubed watermelon rind
4 quarts cold water
1 cup coarse sea salt
9 cups sugar
4 cups distilled (white) vinegar
4 cups water
2 lemons, thinly sliced
4 tsp whole cloves
8 cinnamon sticks broken into 1-inch pieces

Procedure:

Remove the pink flesh and the outermost green rind from the watermelon, and cut the remaining rind into 1-inch cubes. Add the 1 cup of sea salt to the 4 quarts of water to make a brine, and pour this over the cubed watermelon rind in a large bowl. Allow to sit for three hours, then drain and rinse. Put the drained cubes into a large pot, add just enough water to cover, and bring to a simmer. Simmer for 10 minutes, then drain and set the cubes aside.

Make the pickling brine by putting the spices in a spice bag, and add the bag to the mixture of vinegar, water, sugar, and sliced lemon in a medium pot. Bring to a boil, then reduce to a simmer and stir occasionally for half an hour.

Pack the rinds into pint jars, add one of the pieces of cinnamon from the spice bag, cover with hot pickling brine leaving ½ inch of headspace, and process for 15 minutes in a boiling water canner. Allow to sit a month before consuming.

12

Onions

I have it on good authority that, without onions, food would still exist in some form or fashion, but it would hardly be an exaggeration to state that *good* food would be rare. Onions lend their unique flavor and pungency to everything from spaghetti sauce to chicken soup. And along with flavor, they have so many health benefits that even the World Health Organization recognizes them as a medicinal treatment and preventative for chronic diseases.

Onions are well known as a preventative for atherosclerosis, and when used regularly, the fibrinolytic substances they contain suppress the platelet aggregation that can give rise to heart attacks. Several studies have shown that eating as little as half an onion a day reduces the risk of stomach cancer by 40 percent.

Given proper care and conditions and using intensive spacing methods, you will easily reap over 180 onions from a single 4 ft. x 6 ft. bed. The trick lies in the proper care and conditions, along with selecting the right variety for your purposes—so that's what this chapter is all about.

Selecting the Right Variety

Onions can be categorized in a number of different ways. There are bulb-forming and non-bulb-forming onions, sweet and pungent varieties, multiplier onions and seed-bearing onions, and that's just for starters. For now we're just going to discuss the common bulb-forming and seed-bearing onion that people usually grow in their gardens or buy in stores.

This onion, typified by the red, white, and yellow varieties in the grocery store produce department, can be divided into short-day, long-day, and intermediate-day onions based upon how much sunlight they need in order to properly form a bulb. Long-day onions require fifteen or more hours of sunlight, intermediate-day onions require twelve to thirteen hours of sunlight, and short-day onions require only nine to ten hours of sunlight.

The number of hours of sunlight your garden receives at midsummer is determined by your latitude. Though it may be counterintuitive, the closer you are to either the North or South Pole, the greater the hours of sunlight you'll see at midsummer. In practice, this means you can grow a long-day onion in latitudes greater than 40 degrees. In latitudes less than 40 degrees, you'll grow an intermediate-day onion. Short-day onions are used in areas with mild winters and are planted in the fall for a spring harvest.

Not everyone walks around with a globe in his or her back pocket, but there's an easy rule of thumb for the United States. If you are on the East Coast,

Keeping Qualities	Short Day	Intermediate Day	Long Day
Good for storage	Red Creole	Long Yellow Sweet Spanish, California Early Red	White Sweet Spanish, Yellow Sweet Spanish, Walla Walla, Brunswick, Stuttgarter
Best for fresh eating	Bermuda, Grano, Granex, Torpedo, Excel	Yellow Globe, Long Yellow Globe, Candy	Ailsa Craig

Common onion varieties for your location and intended use.

40 degrees runs through Newark, New Jersey, and Pittsburg, Pennsylvania. If you are in the Midwest, it runs through Columbus, Ohio. If you are in the Great Plains, it runs through Lincoln, Nebraska, and Denver, Colorado. If you are on the West Coast, it runs about 100 miles North of Sacramento, California.

The choice of intermediate-day or long-day onion is made for you based on where you live, but there are still other considerations including taste and keeping qualities. When it comes to storage ability, northern growers have a definite advantage. As a general rule, the more pungent a variety, the better it keeps, and long-day onions usually (but don't always) store better than short-day onions. The following table is far from exhaustive, but it lists some common and heirloom onion varieties that are successful in home gardens.

Starting Onions

Onions usually require a long season, so it is a good thing that they are not terribly sensitive to frost. You can start or plant onions in three ways: from seed, from transplants, and from bulbs.

In areas such as Southern California, Georgia, Florida, or Alabama, you can plant seeds in the fall for harvest in the spring. In fact, this is exactly what growers of the famous Vidalia onion do. The Vidalia onion is not its own unique variety, but is rather a Grano or Granex onion that is sweet due to the unique conditions of the soil in that region combined with being grown from seed over the winter months. So if you live in a warmer climate, it could be worthwhile to experiment with growing onions from seed. However, if you live in a cooler climate, you will find that planting onions from seed, even as early as possible in the spring, will give very small bulbs. In this case, you can plant the seeds closely together and use the resultant sprouts (once they are the size of a pencil) as "bunching onions." These are a delightful addition to salads and soups.

In order to form a bulb, onions need to gather a lot of energy from the sun; outside of very warm areas, they will need a head start in order to form a bulb. Thus, onions are typically planted as either bulbs (knows as "sets") or transplants. Onions grown from transplants usually have the best keeping qualities, so if you are growing onions for storage, this is definitely the way to go. Onions should be started indoors approximately 12 weeks before last frost, and the sets planted outside about six weeks before last frost. This gives them the head start they need to form a good bulb. The seeds can be started within a wide temperature range—anywhere from 65 to 80 degrees; once they have sprouted, try to keep them cooler at around 60 degrees for best growth.

Many find growing onions from bulbs to be more convenient, and this can easily be done. Simply sow seeds close together in a small patch of ground about six weeks before last frost. Then, about three or four weeks after midsummer, pull the plants when the bulbs are no more than three-quarters of an inch in diameter. Discard the largest ones or use them for pickling or salads because they will go to seed early if planted. Lay your sets out in the sun (but protect them from rain) for seven to ten days to cure, and then remove the dry tops and store just as you would an onion for eating. Come spring, six weeks prior to last frost, plant them out at their optimal distance for the expected size of that particular variety of onion.

Planting Onions

Soil for onions should already be corrected for the major macronutrients (nitrogen, phosphorus, and potassium) before planting. Raw manures and the like should be strictly avoided, and only very well matured compost employed. This is the case, incidentally, for all root crops that come into direct contact with the soil because fresh manures draw pests, leach nutrients, and, worst of all, lend their flavor to what is grown in them.

⊗ Onions can be started indoors from seed. This technique usually grows the best onions.

⊗ Planting onion bulbs is sometimes more convenient.

The compound in onions that makes them pungent is a sulfur compound. Therefore, onions can be made sweeter by depriving them of sulfur. This, however, can make them keep poorly and be more susceptible to pest damage because sulfur is a crucial element in certain amino acids that are a part of DNA structure. This is why you can only get the famously sweet Vidalia onion during a short time of the year—the low sulfur soil in which it is grown makes it a very poor keeper. Thus, you can make sweeter onions by depriving the soil of sulfur, but you do so at the expense of keeping quality.

Potassium and phosphorus are particularly crucial for onions, and should be present in sufficient quantities prior to planting. If needed, they can be added later in the season as a side dressing in the form of ashes, greensand, bonemeal, etc. Nitrogen, as a key constituent of amino acids, is likewise needed and should be present at adequate levels at the beginning of the season. However, it should not be added later in the season, as doing so will delay or otherwise inhibit the formation of bulbs in favor of excessive top growth. This is where slow-release organic forms of nitrogen, such as alfalfa meal, have a definite advantage over chemicals easily washed from the soil.

Onions taste better when grown in sweeter (i.e., less acidic) soils with pH levels between 6 and 6.8. Lime in either pelleted or powdered form should be applied well in advance of the season because it takes months to affect the pH of the soil. So it is best applied in the fall. If, come spring, the soil pH is still too low, you can use a mixture of powdered lime (which acts slowly) and wood ashes (which act quickly) to raise the pH. These should be mixed into the top six inches of soil very thoroughly as ashes contain potassium hydroxide (wood lye), which can be highly corrosive and therefore toxic to plants in heavy concentrations.

Weeds Are the Nemesis of Onions

Early in the season, onions' greatest vulnerability, due to their slow growth, is being choked out by weeds—particularly grasses. This is especially problematic as distinguishing between an onion and blades of grass can make weeding difficult. As a result, onions are definitely a case for which applying the proverbial "ounce of prevention" is wise.

For beds that will be growing onions, soil solarization as covered in the chapter on weeds is a very effective strategy. This requires some advanced planning because solarization is most effective in July and August when the sun is at its hottest. So you'll need to know in advance which bed you'll be using for onions.

The following step-by-step strategy will allow you to effectively prevent weed problems without the need for chemicals. An added bonus, as part of a bed rotation combined with solarization, nutrients will be more available and diseases will be suppressed.

- Previous spring: Grow a spring crop such as broccoli that is harvested in mid-summer.
- Previous summer: Harvest the spring crop.
- Mix in amendments, then smooth out the bed so it is nice and flat.
- Water the bed very thoroughly with the equivalent of two inches of rain.
- Cover with 6 mil plastic attached to the bed with staples. Leave plastic in place until late August.
- Late August: Remove the plastic and sow with a cover crop.
- Early spring: Harvest cover crop and add to compost pile.
- Cover with dark breathable landscape fabric.
- When the transplants are ready, cut Xs in the landscape fabric and plant them in the Xs.
- Cover the landscape fabric between plants with straw and water thoroughly.

❷ Well-controlled weeds make for happy onions.

Diseases: Rare but Preventable

Though not typically a problem for home gardeners, onions are vulnerable to a number of fungal and bacterial diseases that can be spread via soil; most notable among these diseases are sclerotinia, botrytis, and pinkroot. Primary prevention for these is crop rotation, with pre-solarizing also being a great help.

Sclerotinia of onions shows up as small dark brown spots on the blades that can expand to kill the entire blade while infecting others. The organism responsible is *clerotinia homoeocarpa*, which is the same organism that causes dollar spot on turf grasses, which are its primary host.[1] Using bark mulch or similar mulching to prevent grasses between and around growing beds will help prevent inoculation.

Botrytis infection looks like small white or yellow spots on the blades of the onion where cells have died. These spots appear sunken. Successful infection will usually bring about the death of the tops of the onions in as little as a week. Though botrytis spoors are ubiquitous, the most common source of infection is debris from the prior year's crop where the spoors have overwintered.

1   Saharan, G. & Mehta, N. (2008) *Sclerotinia Diseases of Crop Plants: Biology, Ecology and Disease Management*. ISBN: 978-1-4020-8407-2

In industrial agriculture where onions are grown on a large scale and often re-planted in the same fields year after year, crop losses from botrytis can approach 50 percent annually. However, on the scale of a mini farm, simple preventative measures can keep you from ever seeing it. The conditions that favor development of the mold are cool and wet weather, particularly later in the season. However, this factor alone is insufficient to cause infection. Botrytis spoors require a wound in the onion in order to enter. All you need to do in order to prevent botrytis is the following:

- rotate so that onions aren't grown in the same bed more often than once every four years,
- clear and compost all crop debris at the end of the season so spoors have nowhere to overwinter,
- avoid disturbing the onions during damp or wet weather, and
- respond to the rare pests of onions that can cause breaks in the leaves leaving them vulnerable to infection.

Pinkroot is common in industrial agriculture, but something you will hopefully never see. It manifests in dead onions that die back as though affected by drought, and the bulbs are shriveled and pink. Pinkroot infestation is ubiquitous in poorly drained soils with low levels of organic matter and nutrient deficiencies that have been used to grow onions or other susceptible crops for year after year. The fungus responsible, *Pyrenochaeta terrestris*, is only weakly pathogenic, and if it is infecting your onions, you are doing something wrong.

Using the mini farming method of growing in raised beds, your soil should be well drained, and by using plenty of mature compost for organic matter and rotating crops and amending soil as needed for proper nutrient levels, your onions should be practically invulnerable.

Onion Pests

Most insects don't like to eat onions, and for good reason: when onion tissues are injured, they release a compound that, when mixed with water, produces sulfuric acid. This is why cut onions make your eyes water. But just as there are some intrepid souls who can eat even the most pungent onions as though they were apples, there are a couple of insects who seem not to notice the onion's natural defense mechanism.

Thrips are a common garden pest. They are tiny, with the winged adult being no more than one-tenth of an inch long. Damage from thrips can be twofold: first, through the direct damage they can do to the crop, but most importantly, the cuts they make provide an entry for botrytis. A thrip infestation combined with a week of cold, wet weather can spell doom for the whole crop. They plant their eggs—anywhere from 10 to 100 of them—in the leaves, and when the eggs hatch, the larvae can do considerable damage to the host plant. Thrips are not unique to onions and eat practically anything grown in the garden, so crop rotation won't help.

Prevention requires a combination of cover crop selection, vegetation control, proper soil fertility, and garden hygiene. Clearing crop debris at the end of the season to reduce overwintering populations of thrips is crucial. Their eggs won't survive the composting process. Using a mulch between and around beds to keep extraneous vegetation away will also reduce thrip populations. Thrips have a preference for wheat and rye, so if a cereal grain is anticipated as a cover crop, choose oats instead. Finally, many studies have shown that inadequate levels of calcium as well as trace minerals predispose thrip infestation, so adequate lime plus the addition of sea minerals would be wise. Likewise, excess nitrogen is a risk factor, so maintaining optimal fertility of the soil will ward off this pest.

If all efforts at prevention fail and severe crop damage is likely or occurring, a number of natural insecticides are effective against thrips, including pyrethrin with rotenone, Hot Pepper Wax, and others. Be certain to follow label directions, including safety precautions.

The other likely pest problem is onion maggots, which are the larvae of a fly that lays its eggs near the roots of the plant. The first symptom you'd likely see, as the flies stay hidden, is wilting plants. When you dig them up, you'll find onions that are a rotten and putrid mess. Once an area is infested, it will likely remain so. Meticulous hygiene in debris removal, solarization, and application of parasitic nematodes will help, as will avoiding white onion varieties because these are most susceptible. But of these actions, removal of onion debris, including making sure no onions are left in the ground, is the most important. Overwintering onion maggots need onions for their survival; removing onion debris and burying it deep in the compost pile will substantially reduce their population.

Harvesting Onions

An onion can be pulled and eaten at any stage, but for purposes of storage and marketing, they should be harvested when mature. Onions are mature when

⊗ These onions are ready for harvest!

the tops of 80 percent of them have weakened, turned brown, and flopped over. When this happens, go ahead and bend over the remaining tops, and then allow the onions to remain in the ground until the next sunny day five to ten days away. When harvest day comes, pull up the onions in the morning and leave them outside in the sun until evening. This will kill the little rootlets at the bottom of the bulb. Then bring the onions out of the weather into a place that is shaded, is protected from rain, and has good air circulation. Leave them for a couple of weeks, turning every couple of days. This yields a fully cured onion of the best keeping quality for its variety.

Preparation and Preservation

Whole onions should be stored either braided or in mesh bags with good air circulation in a cool, dark, dry place. Don't let them freeze. Onions can be frozen raw (without blanching) by peeling, quartering, and placing in freezer bags with as much air as possible removed. Onions can also be successfully dehydrated with or

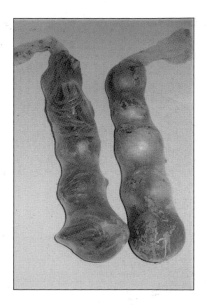

» The onions on the left have sprouted because they were allowed to freeze.

without blanching, but are likely to discolor unless first dipped in a bowl containing 1 cup of water and a tablespoon of lemon juice or a 250 mg vitamin C tablet. The discoloration is harmless and doesn't adversely affect the quality of the onions. Onions can also be pickled in vinegar for preservation using water bath canning; they will turn into a shapeless blob if pressure-canned.

Onions play a key role in food preparation generally, and are prepared in every imaginable way ranging from breaded onion rings to creamed pearl onions.

Dilled Salad Onions

Ingredients:

3 lbs onions, sliced thinly
1½ cups vinegar
1½ cups sugar
3/4 cup water
1 tbsp salt
1½ tsp dill weed

Procedure:

Peel the onions and slice thinly. Pack into sterilized pint jars. Bring the remaining ingredients to a boil and use the resulting pickling mixture to pour into the pint jars leaving ½ inch of headspace. Process in a boiling water bath canner for 15 minutes.

13

Peas

Sometimes kids aren't impressed by peas, but they will likely enjoy classic dishes such as peas with carrots, peas with pearl onions, split pea soup, and more. Naturally, peas fresh out of the garden are far superior to the canned peas from the supermarket, with a bursting sweetness that makes them almost like candy. In addition, peas are high in fiber, protein, vitamin C, vitamin K, and a variety of phytonutrients that make our mothers' advice to eat them quite wise.

Another great thing about peas is that, being legumes, they improve the soil by fixing nitrogen from the air. So using peas (as well as other legumes such as beans) as part of your bed rotation will reduce the need for nitrogen fertilizers.

There are a great many types of peas, representing not just varieties of a given species but also two different species. Garden peas (also known as English peas), which are removed from the pod for eating, and snap peas and snow peas, whose pods are eaten, are members of the species *Pisum sativum*. These peas are a cool-weather crop started in the spring once soil temperatures reach 50 degrees. Split peas are dried peas that have been mechanically split after the shell has been removed.

Cowpeas, also known as black-eyed peas, are members of the species *Vigna unguiculata*; they are adapted to warm seasons and near-drought conditions. Black-eyed peas are usually prepared from a dried state in a fashion identical to dried beans.

Variety Selection

In order to select a variety, you need to determine the type of pea you want to eat. Do you want snow peas for Asian cooking? Sugar snap peas? Shelled garden peas? Split peas for soup? Black-eyed peas?

Among garden peas, my favorites are Laxton's Progress No. 9 and Little Marvel. These are short vines—no more than eighteen inches—that can be very easily trellised around the edges of a bed.

There are now a large variety of sugar snap peas available. My pick of the bunch is a variety known simply as Sugar Snap. These grow a massive six-foot vine requiring a trellis like pole beans.

Flat-podded snow peas are popular in Asian cuisine, and my selection in this category is Oregon Giant. The vines are three feet long, and the pods are harvested while still flat.

I grow the same variety of black-eyed peas that my grandfather grew because I haven't found any varieties I like better. The Black Crowder Cowpea makes an extra-long pod that is easily shelled. At first the peas are purple, but they become black when dried.

Soil Preparation and Planting

Peas prefer deeply worked and well-drained soils with a pH of between 5.8 and 7. You should check macronutrient levels with a soil testing kit and amend as needed with appropriate organic additives. Organic matter is not as important for peas as with other crops, but adding one or two cubic feet of compost per 4 ft. x 8 ft. bed would still be a good idea as it would supply micronutrients as well as biological content that will help assure the success of the inoculant.

Like beans and other legumes, peas perform best when the seeds are treated at planting time with an inoculant containing nitrogen fixing bacteria. The bacteria turn nitrogen from the air into a form usable by peas and other plants and assist with the symbiotic bacterial interface that provides other nutrients to the roots. I put my pea seeds in a pint canning jar, moisten slightly, and then add a heaping tablespoon of inoculant to the jar. The pea seeds are planted after they are swirled around in the jar so they will be evenly coated with inoculant.

Garden, sugar, and snow peas should be planted in the spring as soon as the soil can be worked. This is because the heat of summer shuts them down. If you happen to have apple trees, I have found that the optimal time for planting peas corresponds to the proper time for spring pruning. Otherwise, a soil temperature of 50 degrees is a good guide.

Unlike garden peas, cowpeas are very vulnerable to frost, so they can be planted at the same time as other crops that are susceptible to frost.

Seeds for peas and cowpeas should be planted more deeply than is immediately evident. Usually, seeds are planted at a depth of double the size of the seed, but peas are best planted two inches deep. This is necessary to establish a sufficient root system. If they are planted more shallowly, the plants will be more vulnerable to drought and generally weaker.

Every variety grows a bit differently. Some only grow a vine that is eighteen inches long, so they are easily trellised on a few branches stuck in the ground. (Traditionally these are the branches pruned from fruit trees, though anything other than poison sumac will do fine.) Other varieties might grow as tall as six feet, requiring a more extensive trellis similar to that used for beans. The shorter varieties of peas can be grown around the perimeter of the garden without shading other crops; however, the taller varieties can be grown on the north side of a bed to avoid shading other crops. Peas should be planted at a two-inch interval.

Weeds, Pests, and Diseases

Peas are more vulnerable to weeds than many of their other legume cousins, and because the vines are more delicate, you have to be more careful when weeding. For this reason, I like to get off to a good start by pre-sprouting weeds where peas will be grown, followed by flaming. This way, hand weeding won't be required until the vines are strong and well established.

Pre-sprouting is a straightforward process. You cover a bed with clear plastic in early spring so that it heats more rapidly than it would otherwise, thereby inducing

❮❮ Three rows of peas trellised in a single bed.

weed seeds to sprout. Two weeks is enough. Once that is done, you can dispose of the weeds by hand pulling, using a stirrup hoe, tilling, or flame weeding. Flame weeding offers the advantage of bringing up no new seeds. But if the bed needs to be tilled anyway, the best approach is to till the bed (adding any needed amendments) before the plastic is employed.

Crop rotation between beds and composting all crop debris at the end of the season goes a long way toward keeping disease and pest problems in check. Fusarium wilt and powdery mildew are the most likely diseases to be encountered. Fusarium wilt can be diagnosed by the symptoms: the leaves start browning at the bottom of the plant, and then the disease progresses along the vine's length until the plant is dead. Powdery mildew is aptly named because it appears as a white, powdery mold on the leaves and other plant parts. Thankfully, a large number of pea varieties are resistant to these diseases. Just check the seed catalog when ordering your seeds, and if you have experienced these problems in the past, select resistant varieties.

Though other pests such as Japanese beetles will feed on peas, the primary pests likely to cause difficulties are cutworms, aphids, and slugs.

If you walk out to inspect your garden one morning and find a young seedling snipped off at ground level just as neatly as if it had been done with scissors, you'll know you have a cutworm. The next night, that particular cutworm will get a different plant. Cutworms are little caterpillars about an inch and a half long, usually colored in a motley fashion so that they blend in with the soil. After making a meal of your seedling, the cutworm will usually burrow down into the soil no more than four inches from the seedling and make its bed during the day in preparation for the next night. So if you dig around the cut seedling, you'll dig up the cutworm. My chickens like them, so I save them in a jar along with other grubs, wireworms, and so forth, and feed them to the grateful poultry.

Cutworms can be largely—though not entirely—prevented by timing your planting so that at least two weeks have passed after tilling other organic materials into the ground. For example, if you are cutting a cover crop and tilling it into the ground, wait at least two weeks after incorporating the cover crop before planting the next one, as the fresh organic matter attracts the cutworms.

One thing I have often seen recommended is the use of cardboard collars. This does work, but it can be time-consuming if you are trying to protect fifty plants. There is also a matter of timing in that a cutworm can feed on anything from a new sprout to a transplant as big around as a pencil. The stems expand as the plant grows. So rather than attaching collars directly to plants, it is more efficient to surround them with a wall at the time the seed is planted or the transplant is put in the ground. For this purpose, I use scissors to snip paper towel or toilet paper tubes into 1½-inch sections. You push them into the ground about one-quarter inch around the seed, seedling, or transplant, and you're all set. Eventually they'll become soggy and start to decompose, but by then, danger from cutworms will have passed.

I've mentioned aphids in connection with many plants, and that's because they affect practically every plant to some degree. In most cases their numbers are insufficient to create a problem, so they can be ignored. But if their numbers become too great, they will weaken the plants they infest and predispose those plants to mold or other diseases. If aphids are a problem, they can be dispatched with insecticidal soap sprayed twice, four days apart. Make sure to get under the leaves and along the stems.

Harvest

Garden peas are somewhat like corn in that their sugars will turn to starch if left too long, so the timing of harvest is important. The key is to catch them when they are fully expanded yet immature. Once the pods have started to become round, pick a pod and sample the peas raw every day. The pods on the bottom become ripe first, followed by those on the middle of the vine three days later and those toward the top another three days later. So you'll get three harvests. At the third harvest, just pull up the plant and add it to the compost pile. Once garden peas are harvested, they should be shelled and either eaten or preserved within a couple of hours because from the moment they are picked, their sugars start converting to starch.

Unlike garden peas, the vines of sugar snap peas and snow peas will continue to grow and produce new blooms and pods so long as they are kept harvested. The pods closest to the root are ready first, and once those are ready, count on harvesting every other day until the vines stop producing. Snap peas are harvested when they first start to fatten, but they still snap like a green bean. If you let them stay on the vine longer, the pods will become fibrous and inedible. If this happens, don't despair— just treat it like a garden pea. Snow peas are harvested at an even earlier stage—when the pods are still flat and the peas inside make little lumps no larger than a BB. (The diameter of a BB, incidentally, is 0.177 inches.) Once harvest is started, they need to be harvested daily to keep any pods from becoming overly mature.

Snow peas and sugar snap peas can be stored in a plastic bag in the refrigerator for as long as two weeks without deterioration.

Any of the peas discussed so far can be used as a dried split pea for soup-making. All you need to do is leave the pods on the plant until they turn brown and you can hear the peas rattling when you shake the pod. Pick the pods, and set them aside either in the sun or in a well-ventilated place for a couple of days. Then, split open the pod by pressing on the seam and remove the peas. You can split the peas as you go along by using a thumbnail, and the work progresses pretty quickly. It's the sort of thing you can do if forced to watch a bad movie on television with a family member. Put the split peas in a large bowl and allow to sit out for a couple of weeks to dry, mixing with your hand every once in a while. Then, store them in an airtight container in a cool place away from sunlight.

Cowpeas or black-eyed peas are treated the same as split peas. Harvest when the pods are brown and you can hear the peas rattling when you shake the pod.

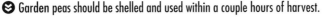 Garden peas should be shelled and used within a couple hours of harvest.

Preparation and Preservation

As I explained above, garden peas should be shelled and then eaten or preserved as soon as possible after harvest to preserve their sweetness. Split peas and cowpeas should be harvested when the pods are brown. Shell, and then allow them to dry before being stored in an airtight container. Sugar snap and snow peas can be sealed in a plastic bag and kept in the refrigerator for up to two weeks without loss of quality.

Garden peas, sugar snap, and snow peas are all at their best fresh, but they freeze very well. Steam blanch garden peas for 2½ minutes or edible podded peas for 4 minutes. Dump them into ice water for an equal amount of time to cool, dry them, and then seal in freezer bags with as much air removed as possible.

Sesame Snow Peas
Ingredients:

1 lb snow peas
1 tbsp sesame seeds
2 tbsp canola oil
1 tbsp toasted sesame seed oil
2 tsp soy sauce
½ tsp ground ginger
4 green onions, chopped small
2 carrots, julienned

Procedure:

Prepare the snow peas by pinching off the stem end and pulling the strings down the pod. (Strings may not be present depending upon pea variety and timing of harvest.) Toast the sesame seeds in a dry pain, stirring constantly over low heat for 5 minutes. Set the toasted sesame seeds aside. Bring a large skillet to high heat, add the oils, then add the remaining ingredients. Keep in constant motion so nothing burns (peas burn easily due to their high sugar content) until the peas are a bright green and slightly tender. Then add the soy sauce, put in the sesame seeds, give everything another good stir, and then transfer to a heated dish for serving.

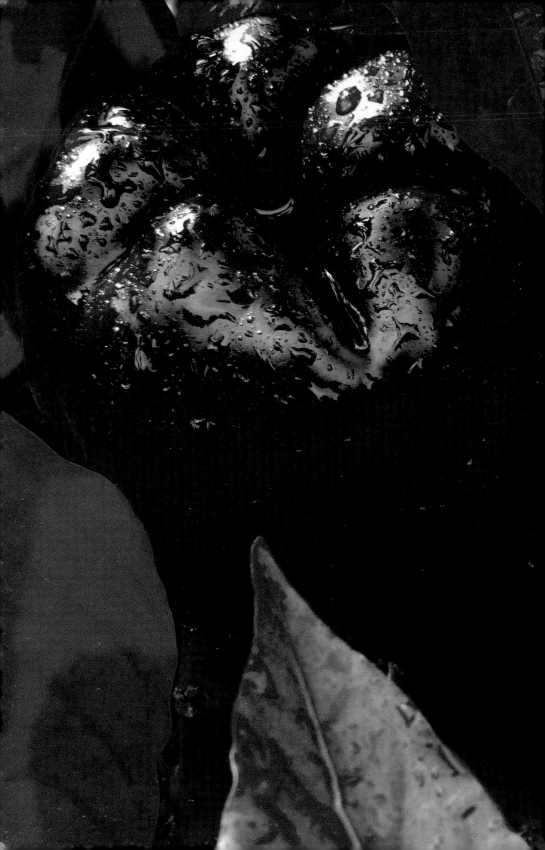

14

Peppers

Native to Mexico, South America, and Central America, peppers have become an important ingredient in cuisines worldwide, both in the form of sweet peppers and hot peppers. The peppers available in the store represent only a tiny fraction of the range of this versatile fruit, and growing your own peppers is an ideal way to experience the array of flavors available. A cup of ripe sweet peppers contains two days' supply of vitamin C and more than a day's supply of vitamin A, along with a good dose of vitamin B6, fiber, and important antioxidants.

Peppers can be divided into two broad categories: sweet and hot. Sweet peppers carry two copies of a recessive gene that inhibits the production of the capsaicin and closely related compounds that give hot peppers their bite. Many sweet peppers have been bred, and the standard blocky bell pepper is the one with which most people are familiar, though there are many other sweet pepper cultivars that have a wide array of shapes, flavors, and colors.

Hot peppers either lack the gene that inhibits capsaicin or have only one copy of the gene. Because the gene is recessive, with only one copy (rather than two), capsaicin production is not inhibited. Open-pollinated hot peppers always lack the gene altogether, but in some hybrids there is only one copy. Once capsaicin production is enabled, however, there are other genes that modulate the amount that is produced in a given variety of hot pepper as well as genes that have the effect of creating different flavors and colors.

The degree of hotness of a pepper is measured in either Scoville heat units or ASTA pungency units. The Scoville heat units are a measure of how much an alcoholic extract of the dried pepper must be diluted before it is just barely detectable by a panel of five tasters; the larger the number, the hotter the pepper. ASTA pungency units are derived through use of High Performance Liquid Chromatography (HPLC) to measure the absolute amount of capsaicinoid content. Most people are familiar with the Scoville Heat Units and, in my personal opinion, because there are elements to taste outside of just a specific set of related chemicals, SHUs are a better measure of a person's likely subjective reaction.

The peperoncini peppers on a Greek salad and the pimentos stuffed into olives usually have fewer than 200 Scoville Heat Units, so they are pretty mild. Banana peppers will have up to 500 SHUs. Jalapeño peppers will have more than 2,500 SHUs. The world's hottest pepper is the Naga Viper, with more than 1,300,000 SHUs.

This little yellow pepper is mildly hot.

Variety Selection

Peppers are indigenous to warm zones with long growing seasons, though over time, varieties have been selected that will do fine in cooler zones with shorter seasons. So the most important aspect of a cultivar to consider is its growing season. Keep in mind that there are two maturity dates for peppers: one for green peppers and another for ripe peppers. Usually a catalog listing will give the number of days for green peppers and then specify an additional number of days for those peppers to ripen. Especially if you plan to save seeds, you want to choose a variety whose time to a mature and fully ripen fruit is at least ten days less than the length of your growing season. My area only has ninety-six frost-free days on average, so I have to pick varieties that are ripe in eighty-six days or less.

Another consideration is whether you prefer peppers that are sweet or hot and whether the peppers are for use in salads, salsa, frying, or other specific uses.

Because my mini farm is in the Northeast, my particular choices might not be the best for other parts of the country, so you can use these as a starting point only for your own experimentation: I grow Jimmy Nardello's both for frying and drying, Ozark Giant or California Wonder for salads, and Black Hungarian as a hot pepper for salsas and spice. This latter is about half as hot as a jalapeño and has a nice smoky flavor.

Starting and Planting

Peppers should be started indoors seven weeks before last frost and planted out a week after last frost after they have two sets of true leaves. They germinate slowly at lower temperatures, so use a heat mat when growing seedlings indoors to achieve the best temperature of 70 to 80 degrees. In addition, make sure to keep the fluorescent lights to within an inch of the leaves so the stems are stocky and strong. In order to avoid bacterial leaf spot (unless you are planting a variety of pepper that is resistant to that disease), the seed should be pretreated via the

method described in the section on weeds, pests, and diseases.

Prepare the bed for the peppers by correcting the pH to between 6.0 and 6.5, thoroughly incorporating three cubic feet of finished compost or well-rotted manure per 4 ft. x 8 ft. bed. Correct the soil for the major macronutrients and then add an additional two pounds of bonemeal per 4 ft. x 8 ft. bed.

When transplanting, sprinkle a tablespoon of Epsom salt (magnesium sulfate) into the hole that will receive the

A frying pepper awaiting my frying pan. ❯❯

transplant and mix it into the soil. Space transplants at twelve inches to eighteen inches. Water transplants daily for the first week and then make sure they get the equivalent of an inch of rain every week in the form of a deep soaking rather than multiple shallow waterings.

Weeds, Pests, and Diseases

Because peppers are spaced a good distance apart, if you make sure the bed is weed-free before planting, weeds can be either handpicked or controlled by carefully using a stirrup hoe.

Bacterial leaf spot (BLS) is an economically important disease of peppers that has caused failure of entire crops. It starts with water-soaked spots on leaves that turn brown. Subsequently, the affected leaf may turn yellow, wither, and die. The reduced foliage reduces yield and delays fruit maturity, and the spots can affect the peppers as well. BLS is spread primarily via infected seeds, though once the infection is present it will inhabit the soil and can be spread from plant to plant, especially in wet conditions, via hand contact. Once an infection is noticed, it can be controlled and kept from spreading by applying copper sulfate as indicated on the package. If you run into trouble with bacterial leaf spot, keep in mind that crop rotation and thoroughly cleaning up crop debris at the end of season are the best preventatives. If that is insufficient, pretreating seeds and growing resistant cultivars will help.

Seeds can be pretreated with scalding water to kill the bacteria. Unfortunately, this is a delicate process because the bacteria are inside the seed, so anything that would kill the bacteria would adversely affect the vigor of the seed as well. Ideally, this would be accomplished using laboratory equipment such as stirring hot plates and so forth, but the gear to do that would easily cost $400. Thankfully, there is another way that is a lot less expensive. The only gear you'll need that you may not already have is a high quality laboratory-grade thermometer such as the Fisher Scientific 14-983-15B.

Seed Pre-treatment
Ingredients/Equipment:

3 large Styrofoam coffee cups
1 fitted lid for one of the coffee cups
1 saucepan with 8 cups water
1 quart jar cool water, uncovered

2 ice cubes
1 laboratory grade thermometer with a Fahrenheit scale
1 clean handkerchief, cut in four squares (use one of the squares)
2 rubber bands
1 large nut

Procedure:

1. Nest two of the coffee cups together and set the lid next to them. These are for the hot water.
2. Fill the other coffee cup two-thirds full with cold water and add the two ice cubes.
3. Twist the nut into a pocket in the square of handkerchief, and secure with a rubber band. Put the seeds in an adjacent pocket formed similarly, and secure with the other rubber band.
4. Bring the water in the pot to a temperature of exactly 122 degrees F. Test by swirling the water with the thermometer and observing the reading. If the temperature goes higher than 122 degrees, turn off the burner and add cool water a little at a time, stirring each time until the temperature is exactly 122 degrees.
5. Pour the water from the pot into the two nested cups until two-thirds full.
6. Add the handkerchief and assure that it sinks.
7. Attach the lid.
8. Wait 25 minutes.
9. Remove the handkerchief from the hot water, put it in the cup containing ice water, and leave it there for another 25 minutes.
10. Removed the handkerchief, unwrap the seeds, dry them on paper towels, and plant as usual.

Phytophthera root rot, also known as "chile wilt," occurs throughout the United States but is most economically important in irrigated fields. The conditions that give rise to it—"wet feet" or waterlogged soil—simply do not exist in raised beds. Furthermore, as it is caused by a microorganism, standard sanitation and rotation practices will keep it even further suppressed, so you are unlikely to ever encounter this problem on your mini farm.

There are about twenty other bacterial and viral diseases that could theoretically infect your peppers, but just as with phytophthera, standard mini farming practices will make most of them a theory rather than a fact. The one exception is tobacco mosaic virus (TMV). TMV can be present in the tobacco in cigarettes, and it is easily transmitted by hand to peppers, tomatoes, potatoes, and other plants in that family. If anyone who touches your plants smokes, uses snuff, etc., make sure he washes his hands thoroughly before touching the plants. Other viruses, such as tobacco etch virus, and pepper mosaic, are transmitted by aphids. If you keep aphids controlled, the lawn mowed, and border weeds well away from your garden, these are an unlikely problem.

Aphids are a pest of all pepper species. Because of their role in transmitting diseases in peppers, you want to keep them under control. Aphids are a small, soft-bodied insect, green for camouflage, and they are usually kept controlled by natural predators. You can often prevent them by growing a bed of something they really like, such as marigolds, at some distance from the crop you are trying to protect. (This is called a trap crop.) But if they become prolific, you can keep them controlled by spraying weekly with a dilute solution (one tablespoon per gallon of water) of pure soap such as Dr. Bronner's or a specific insecticidal soap.

Slugs can also be an issue. You'd think, especially with hot peppers, that slugs would avoid them, but evidently they have no taste and will eat foliage and the peppers alike. Ground up eggshells combined with coffee grounds (renewed every couple of weeks) will create a deadly barrier around your pepper plants. The coffee grounds are poisonous to them and the eggshells cut their skin so they dehydrate. Other ways to deal with slugs are explained in Chapter 9: Greens.

Root-knot nematodes are microscopic roundworms that can affect many garden plants, including peppers. Symptoms include wilting and loss of productivity. When the plants are pulled, the roots have little nodules that can be as big as a pea, though they are usually smaller. Root-knot nematodes prefer sandy soils low in organic matter, so if you use plenty of cured compost to start with, they won't likely become a problem. Use plenty of compost, practice crop rotation, pull up and compost old pepper plants, and you won't have trouble.

Pepper maggots are the larvae of a fly with green eyes and a yellow head that is the same size as an ordinary housefly. The female uses an ovipositor to punch a hole in the surface of the pepper and then lays a tiny egg that grows into a white-yellow larva a bit under half an inch long. The larva eats inside the pepper, burrows back out, falls to the ground, and then pupates in the soil. The injury to the fruit opens it up to diseases, and the insides become discolored. Pepper maggots aren't a problem for thin-skinned hot peppers, but they do tend to adversely affect sweet bell peppers. Keep in mind that you can grow peppers for years without seeing a pepper maggot and then suddenly have an entire crop wiped out. Remedies are the usual: sanitation and rotation. Sanitation in the form of burying old/dead/rotting peppers deep in the compost pile is particularly important because it is the scent of rotting peppers that draws the adult flies.

Harvest

Peppers can be harvested at any stage, though hot and sweet peppers alike have more sweetness and flavor when harvested fully ripe.

Each pepper plant has what is called a "fruit load." This is the maximum number of peppers that the plant can sustain given its foliage and root system. Once a plant has reached its fruit load, it will cease to flower or produce new fruits. In general, then, it is best to harvest some early fruits while green to make room for more peppers and to allow some of these latter peppers to stay through full maturity and ripening.

Peppers vary in color as they ripen. Some ripen to orange and others to red or even purple. A good rule of thumb is the less green you see on the pepper, the more ripe it is. Once they start to lose their green color, they ripen quickly—sometimes in just a day or two. Peppers start to lose quality quickly once fully ripe, so keep an eye on them and harvest when ready. Letting a pepper stay on the plant overlong does not improve its flavor. If you are planning to can or pickle your peppers, they maintain their crispness better when harvested a day or two prematurely.

The stems of pepper plants are brittle and delicate. You can harvest peppers, especially when ripe, just by lifting up the fruit; fruit stem will separate from the plant easily enough. But when the peppers are green, this happens with difficulty and there is the possibility of breaking the plant stems. So I use a pair of garden sheers to cut the fruit stem with minimal disturbance to the plant.

As noted previously, hot peppers contain an oily substance called capsaicin. Capsaicin can wreak havoc on mucus membranes at even low concentrations and burn or blister skin at higher concentrations. In fact, law enforcement officers use the substance to disable people resisting arrest, so it is pretty powerful stuff. When harvesting hot peppers, resist any urge to scratch your nose or rub your eyes. If your skin starts to burn, you can remove the capsaicin from your skin (but NOT eyes, nose, etc.!) with rubbing alcohol. Internally, milk can be helpful

Seed Saving

Peppers are both self-fertile (meaning they will self-pollinate from the male and female parts inside the same flower and that they are receptive to their own pollen), and can be insect-pollinated. All peppers are the same species, so they will interbreed freely. If you are planning to save seed, you either have to practice isolation techniques or grow only one variety of pepper. Isolation is as simple as covering the flower with a bag made from spun polyester. (Floating row cover is made from spun polyester; this is plentiful and cheap.) Cover the flower before it opens and gently shake the plant a couple of times a day to encourage self-pollination. Once a fruit starts to form, remove the bag but mark that pepper as one that will be used for seeds.

Pepper seeds have greater vigor and higher germination rates if the peppers from which they are taken are allowed to become overripe. Allow the marked peppers to mature for an extra week or two after becoming fully ripe.

Seeds are collected by cutting open the pepper and removing them. Put the seeds, separated from any internal membranes, on a paper plate and allow them to dry for a month. Then dehydrate further over a silica gel desiccant and store in a sealed container in a cool place away from sunlight.

Preparation and Preservation

Peppers can be eaten raw or cooked. They will keep in the refrigerator for one or two weeks in sealed plastic bags, and can be pickled, canned, dehydrated, and frozen.

For freezing and dehydrating, first blanch the peppers in water (two minutes for rings, three minutes for halves) or steam (three minutes for rings, five minutes for halves) and then cool in ice water for several minutes. Then the peppers can be blotted dry and either frozen in evacuated freezer bags or dehydrated and stored in airtight jars.

Un-pickled peppers must be pressure-canned. But pickled peppers can be canned in a water bath canner. In either case, the process of canning makes the skin tough, so the skin is best removed. The skin is removed via a process known as "blistering." This consists of heating the skin, causing it to be easily removed. You can do this in the microwave, oven, or frying pan. To use the frying pan method, cut off the top and bottom of the peppers, split them lengthwise, and remove the seeds. Heat the pan to medium. Put the split peppers in the pan skin-side down until the skins start to blister. Allow the peppers to cool and then peel off the skin.

Though it varies with the variety of pepper, sometimes you can skip blistering by steam blanching the peppers for four minutes first, which sufficiently softens the skin. You can try it both ways and note the difference. In general, if I am cutting up the peppers small for a relish, I blanch them; if I am leaving them long, I blister them.

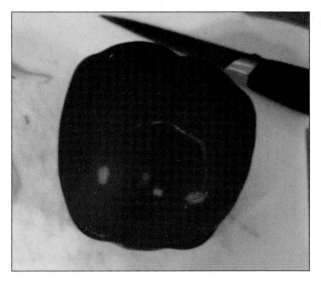

These striations occur most often on hot peppers, but if you see them, harvest immediately so the pepper isn't overripe.

Pickled Peppers

Ingredients:

8 lbs peppers (cleaned, seeds removed, sliced lengthwise and blistered or blanched)

7 cups vinegar (5% acetic acid—either cider vinegar or distilled vinegar is fine)

1 1/3 cups water

2 tbsp pickling salt

3 tbsp sugar

2 cloves garlic

1 tsp peppercorns

1 tsp whole coriander seeds

Procedure:

Prepare the peppers. (They can be hot, sweet, or a mix.) Combine the remaining ingredients in a large saucepan to make the brine, bring to a boil, and allow to simmer for 10 minutes. Pack the peppers into sterilized jars leaving one inch of headspace; then fill the jars with brine leaving ½ inch of headspace. Adjust the two-piece caps, and process in a boiling water canner for 10 minutes. Makes 8–9 pints.

15

Potatoes

Originating in the Andes mountains and spread across the globe by European explorers, potatoes have become a staple crop throughout the world. In fact, though you are unlikely to find potatoes at a Chinese or Indian restaurant, China and India are the world's first- and third-ranked producers of potatoes, respectively. Potatoes are calorically dense, easy to grow, delicious, and packed with vitamin C, potassium, vitamin B6, and fiber.

Potatoes also contain what is called resistant starch. This is starch that can't be broken down into sugars by enzymes in the small intestine and is instead fermented in the large intestine. Research indicates that this resistant starch helps in the synthesis of important short-chain fatty acids and acts as a probiotic encouraging the growth of beneficial bacteria in the colon. Potatoes, especially purple and red ones, contain a substantial amount of antioxidants as well.

Because of the glycemic index[1] of potatoes and the growing problem with weight management in the United States, there are many who would counsel not to eat potatoes (or any other concentrated carbohydrate such as grains or breads) for reasons of health. This subject is fiercely debated by experts, and I'm not about to definitively address the issue in a book on gardening. Instead, I will point out that the glycemic index of a potato is influenced by the variety grown, where it is grown, and even how it is prepared.

Potatoes are a member of the nightshade family, and the foliage and fruits of potato plants are poisonous, containing a number of toxic compounds. Solanine is the toxic compound most likely to be a concern for humans.

In general, the actual tubers of potato plants contain a safely low concentration of solanine. However, there are two circumstances where this may not be true. If potatoes are exposed to light, their skin starts to turn green and solanine concentrations within the tuber increase rapidly. Do not eat any potatoes with green skin! If you live in South America, there are some wild closely related species that have toxic tubers. If you grow potatoes from true seed in such an area, be sure to use isolation practices. Otherwise, the plants grown from the true seed could yield a toxic potato. This is not an issue in the United States or Europe as toxic wild potatoes don't grow in those areas.

There is also some concern about acrylamide—a suspected carcinogen in tobacco smoke. The problem is that acrylamide is formed in carbohydrate-rich foods when they are cooked,[2] and can provide a level of acrylamide exposure similar to smoking. If this is a matter of concern for you, two things can be done to lessen the amount of acrylamide derived from eating potatoes. First, do not eat stored potatoes once they have become soft. This softness comes from the starch turning to sugar, and the higher sugar content leads to higher acrylamide formation on cooking. The second is to cook potatoes by first boiling and then cooling them for consumption. This decreases the amount of acrylamide formed and simultaneously increases the amount of beneficial resistant starch.

---

1   Glycemic index is a measure of how much a person's blood sugar levels are raised by eating food. The higher the glycemic index, the more (or more quickly) the blood glucose level is raised.
2   Tarake, E. et. al. (2002) *J Agric Food Chem.* 2002 Aug 14;50(17):4998-5006.

Variety Selection

Though there are literally thousands of varieties of potatoes, only a few dozen are commercially available. The primary consideration in choosing a potato cultivar is the purpose for which the potatoes will be used. Different varieties of potatoes have different amounts of starch as well as different ratios of amylose and amylopectin. High levels of starch create qualities desirable in a baking potato, high levels of amylose are best in mashed potatoes, and higher levels of amylopectin allow for better boiled potatoes for potato salads. All of these characteristics are different for each variety of potato, so it is best to select a variety suitable for the end use.

Potatoes are also susceptible to a number of diseases including late blight, scab, verticillium wilt, potato viruses, black spot and more. For most of these diseases, resistant varieties have been bred. If you have difficulty with a given disease, look in the seed catalogs to see what resistant varieties are available.

Starting and Planting

Potatoes can be started either from tubers or true botanical seeds. By far the most popular method is using the tubers. The eyes that form on potatoes are a small plant that, if planted in soil and allowed to grow, will turn into a full potato plant that will grow more potatoes.

Potatoes can accumulate many blights and viral diseases that can be passed in the tubers. For this reason, using potatoes from the supermarket is a very bad idea. Will it work? Usually it will. I've done it. But just because I've done something foolish and gotten away with it, that doesn't mean it should be emulated. The fact is that potatoes in the supermarket are not screened for diseases, and using them as seed stock can be a recipe for crop failure.

	Baking	Mashed	Salad
Early/New Potatoes	All Blue, Purple Viking, Red Gold	German Butterball, Mountain Rose, Red Gold	Red Pontiac, Nicola, Sangre
Main Crop	Burbank Russet, Gold Rush, Katahdin	Burbank Russet, Kennebec	Yukon Gold, Yellow Finn, La Ratte

There are a great many sources for Certified Seed Potatoes. These are grown in isolation and tested for diseases. You can use them on your farm with a high degree of confidence that you aren't importing something nasty.

In terms of productivity, Certified Seed Potatoes are usually superior to true botanical seed. Seed potatoes are cloned from the most productive plants available to the seed producer, whereas the results of heterosexual reproduction in true seed never reproduce either parent's characteristics exactly. So using seed potatoes that have been certified disease-free from a reputable supplier is generally most productive in the short term.

Nevertheless, I recommend growing potatoes from true botanical seed because most of the potatoes commercially available are from just a handful of cloned varieties representing a tiny segment of genetic diversity that leaves our food supply far more vulnerable than it should be to unknown pest and disease threats. True botanical seed gives and preserves the greatest genetic diversity, giving greater odds of maintaining a crop in the face of unknown future hazards. Furthermore, it gives you the ability to save your own seeds to cut costs and increase self-sufficiency.

Potatoes grow best in loose soil that is rich in organic matter, so mix in two to four cubic feet of well-finished compost per 4 ft. x 8 ft. bed. Don't use immature compost or fresh animal feces as these can suck certain nutrients out of the soil and impart off-flavors and potential human pathogens to the crop. Further-

more, fresh manures can cause unsightly scab on potatoes. Potatoes will grow fine in soils with a pH as low as 4.8, and in fact these lower pH levels inhibit the fungus that causes scab, so skip the lime. Beyond that, if you add micronutrients (including boron) and correct the soil levels of macronutrients using appropriate organic amendments, you'll be

« These Certified Seed Potatoes are ready for planting.

fine. Potatoes also need soil to be well drained, but using raised beds solves that problem in advance.

Potatoes are a cool weather crop and should be planted about a month before the last frost. This is important, as the productivity of potatoes falls in 90-degree weather, and 95-degree weather may even kill the plants. So get started early!

If you use true botanical seed rather than seed potatoes, start those seeds indoors ten weeks before last frost so they can be planted outside at four weeks before last frost. Plant twice as many seeds as you think you'll need because germination rates on true seed aren't very good. If using Certified Seed Potatoes, set them in a warm window for a week in advance of planting to help them break dormancy. Small- and medium-sized seed potatoes can be planted whole, but large ones should be cut into sections with at least two buds in each section. Allow the cut potatoes to scab over in the open air for a day before planting. Plant either the seed potatoes or the transplants grown from true seed at eighteen-inch intervals in all directions. If your beds are so narrow you can only fit in two rows at that distance, you can space the seed potatoes or transplants at one foot lengthwise and allow two feet between those rows. Plant the transplants as you would any other, and put seed potatoes two to three inches underground.

When the plants have grown to six inches, mound the dirt over them and let them grow some more. This will maximize the total number of potatoes grown from each plant. There are limits to this method: the plants need foliage to make tubers, and the more stem you put underground, the less foliage there is to make tubers. I have tried mounding potatoes as high as two feet and have found their productivity to be no greater than in instances where I have planted the seed potatoes two inches deep in a six-inch trench and then filled in the trench with more dirt once the potato plants had grow up above the edge of the trench. You can continue mounding up until the plants start to flower, at which point new tubers stop being produced.

Potatoes need sufficient water to prevent hollow tubers and to grow them to optimal sizes. The equivalent of one inch of water weekly is sufficient.

Weeds, Pests, and Diseases

Potato vines grow quickly. Planted as closely as I've recommended, all you need to do is make sure all of the weeds in the bed are pulled prior to planting, and the vines will shade out competition in short order. All that will remain is keeping weeds at the edge of the bed pulled before they set seed.

Potatoes have a few pests. Colorado potato beetles are pretty much a given anytime you plant potatoes. Wireworms can be a serious problem, especially in areas that abut or were previously grass. These two are the most likely to be of economic importance, but you can also experience damage from flea beetles, aphids, and cutworms.

Colorado potato beetles and their larvae eat the foliage of potato plants. A single female can lay hundreds of eggs, so if left unchecked, just a couple of beetles can devastate a crop in a couple of weeks. When the beetles are done with the potatoes, they may also jump to any eggplant or tomato plants they can find. The adult beetles are up to three-eighths of an inch long, are bright yellow or orange, and have five distinct brown stripes on each wing. They lay yellow eggs underneath the leaves in clusters of thirty, which hatch in a few days. The larvae are reddish-orange with a row of black spots on each side.

In practice, because of their high fecundity, natural predators are almost always insufficient to keep potato beetles in check even using the best practices. The only alternatives available are to grow a resistant variety of potato (such as King Harry, Dakota Diamond, or Elba) or spray them with something that will kill potato beetles.

Adult potato beetles overwinter just under the ground, so in large-scale operations the practices of flaming, plastic trenches, and similar physical controls have an aggregate effect that can mitigate the need for spraying when combined with crop rotation involving fields separated by long distances. Unfortunately, in a small-scale operation like a mini farm, crop rotation doesn't give enough separation. And, if you flame the beds in which potatoes were previously grown, the beetles arrive anyway from alternate natural hosts such as horse nettle or woody

❰❰ Colorado potato beetles are an important pest of potatoes.

nightshade (two common weeds). Thus, if resistant varieties aren't grown, we are left with spraying.

When spraying for Colorado potato beetles, I use a three-part mix that includes natural pyrethrin, rotenone, and spinosad, each added in concentrations specified by the manufacturers. Pyrethrin is a contact poison highly toxic to bees, so spray it at dusk once all bees have left your plants to avoid hurting them. Its effects last a couple of days before it is rendered harmless through fresh air and sunshine.

Rotenone is an organic poison from the roots of certain tropical plants. It needs to be ingested to work and will last on plants for up to six days. Pyrethrin and rotenone are both neurotoxins, but they work in different ways so that when combined, resistance is less likely to develop. Both of these poisons target the adult beetles to keep them from laying more eggs and stop them from doing damage, though they will also kill any larvae. Spinosad is a bacterial toxin derived from a unique bacteria found in a rum distillery in the 1980s. It has to be ingested, and is especially toxic to larvae. It takes a couple of days to kill the larvae, but they stop feeding immediately. I have found full control with only two sprayings a week apart.

Wireworms are a serious problem for potatoes as well as carrots, parsnips, beets, Jerusalem artichokes, and practically any other edible root save those in the onion family. Wireworms will also damage directly planted corn seeds. They will be in soil that was previously lawn or is near lawn. Grassy cover crops such as rye will likewise attract them. Rotations with crops they don't like, such as mustard or onions, have no practical effect in reducing their presence.

Up until soil temperatures reach 60 degrees, as many as a quarter of wireworms are two or three feet underground—far deeper than you will dig. But once the soil temperatures are that high, the preponderance of the wireworm population will be in the top one foot of soil. Though poisoning them is the modus operandi in industrial agriculture, the poisons used are among the most toxic imaginable and often require special permits for use as some of them, such as chlorpicrin and methyl bromide, are chemical warfare gases usable as weapons of mass destruction. Others, such as carbofuran and imidacloprid, are systemic insecticides that are absorbed into the plant tissues of the treated crop, which is a valid cause for concern.

Obviously, I'm not going to encourage this approach on a mini farm. What I do, as part of preparing a bed for potatoes or any other root crop, is dig through the soil looking for wireworms with a fine-tooth comb. As I find them, I put them in a jar, and when I'm done, I feed them to the chickens. Also, prior to planting I turn the chickens loose in the yard. They inevitably forage through the beds pulling weeds and eating various bugs, including wireworms. This is not 100 percent effective, but over time it has reduced crop damage to tolerable levels.

With potatoes, another very viable approach is to grow them in containers. As long as there are holes in the bottom (blocked with a water-permeable barrier that will exclude wireworms) to allow for drainage, growing potatoes in containers such as five-gallon buckets is entirely feasible and works well.

Potatoes are susceptible to several economically important diseases, including early blight, late blight, scab, and black leg. Black leg is not a problem in raised beds because they provide adequate drainage to prevent the disease. The most important weapon against the other diseases is crop rotation such that the same bed is not used to grow anything from the nightshade family (potato, tomato, pepper, eggplant, etc.) any more often than once every four years. Spoors also overwinter in crop debris and culled potatoes; crop debris and culled potatoes should be routinely buried deeply in the hottest section of the compost pile.

Early blight affects potatoes and tomatoes. It is caused by *Alternaria solani* and shows up first on the lowest leaves of the plant; it can ultimately kill the entire plant and adversely affect the tubers. It starts as a small, sunken brown spot on the

❤ This stackable frame with a landscape fabric bottom allows potatoes to be progressively hilled and excludes wireworms.

leaf and then expands. Usually, there is more than one such spot. As the spot progresses, the leaf turns yellow, then brown, and dies. In my experience, this disease will also affect cabbage-family crops once it is in the soil, so make sure to rotate crops such that nothing in either the nightshade or cabbage family is grown in that bed for four years to help deny it a host.

One thing that can help with this problem, as the fungus usually affects leaves rather than stems, is to grow your potato vines on a trellis and remove any leaves within one foot of the ground. This method minimizes opportunities for the fungal spoors to be splashed up onto the lower foliage by rain or watering. I have also completely avoided this problem by planting my potatoes in an established living clover cover crop.

If all else fails and early blight visits your potatoes anyway, you can spray with a *Bacillus subtilis*-based preparation used according to label directions starting as soon as the infection is noticed, and this will usually control the disease.

Like early blight, late blight also affects tomatoes. Late blight is also known as potato blight and was the disease responsible for the Irish potato famine. The water-soaked areas on the leaves that serve as the first symptom usually escape notice, but those areas then turn brown and, as the leaf dies, turn black. The spoors are washed from the leaves into the soil where they infect the tubers. Warm, wet weather favors its growth, and you may see gray hairy mold growing under affected leaves in humid weather. Crop rotation is very important to prevent this disease and, because the spoors overwinter on potatoes left in the soil, plants growing in cull piles, and so forth, meticulous sanitation is equally valuable.

Yet, in spite of the best rotation and sanitation, some of the spoors may blow into your beds; if they take hold, it can be a serious problem. Sprays are more effective as preventatives than curatives, and those with greatest utility in that regard are copper sulfate and *Bacillus subtilis*. A program of regular spraying, at least once every fourteen days with particular attention to getting the undersides of the leaves is generally effective. Copper can accumulate in the soil and reach toxic

levels, so I would generally recommend using the *Bacillus subtilis* instead; it is also more effective. If you see signs of infection in the plants, you can mix both together as the mixture is synergistic. If you

≪ The symptoms of early blight when it starts on the lower leaves are distinctive.

grow a large crop of potatoes and you see some of them are affected, you can cut off the affected plants immediately and burn or thermophilically compost them. This will often stop the spread of infection.

Potato scab is another fungus. It leaves unsightly scab-like blemishes on the surface of potatoes but doesn't pose a risk to the plant overall, and the potatoes, once peeled, are perfectly edible. Even so, it makes the potatoes unsellable. The best preventative is to grow the potatoes in beds where the pH is lower than 5.2; the fungus that causes scab doesn't survive well below that pH but the potatoes will do just fine. This, however, may not be practical as crops are rotated between beds and most crops prefer a pH of 6 or higher. If lowering the pH that much is not practical, a rotation of at least three years substantially diminishes scab. Using plenty of compost to enrich the soil provides competitive organisms that diminish the incidence of scab even further.

Harvest

As long as they are not green, which indicates the presence of poisonous solanine, potatoes can be harvested at any stage. Early or so-called "new" potatoes can be harvested a week after the potato plants start to flower. New potatoes do not keep well, so they must be used soon after harvest. If you are careful, you can gently dig around under the plants with your bare hands and take a few new potatoes and leave the plants otherwise undisturbed. The potatoes that remain will continue to mature.

Or, you can pull up entire plants and dig around. Because the soil in my beds is uncompressed and practically ideal, I can harvest with my hands and nothing more than a garden trowel. If your beds aren't yet at the point, you can use a digging fork. Stick it in the dirt twelve to sixteen inches from the base of the plant, making sure to insert it as deeply as possible, and then lean back using the digging fork as a lever until the tines emerge from the soil. Do this along one side of the plants and then along the other side, and then dig out the potatoes with your hands.

This same technique is applicable when harvesting fully mature potatoes. Fully mature potatoes have a toughened skin and are more suitable for long-term storage. Potatoes are mature when the foliage starts to die back later in the season. In my area, that is usually late August.

Mature potatoes harvested this way should be harvested in the morning, laid out in the sun to dry, and then turned at midday for even sun exposure. After that, the dirt can be brushed off with a large clean paint brush and the potatoes can be stored.

Seed Saving

If you use tubers to start your potatoes, you are best off not trying to use your own tubers as seed potatoes except in an emergency because, as I mentioned earlier, a number of diseases will tend to accumulate, and within just a couple of years you are likely to have seemingly intractable disease issues. So if you use tubers, you should order or otherwise obtain Certified Seed Potatoes every year.

I have previously discussed using true botanical potato seed as the only practical way for a mini farmer to save potato seeds at all without concentrating diseases. So if total self-sufficiency is your goal, using true seed—even if productivity may be a bit less—is the way to go.

If you are going to grow your potatoes from true seed, it would be best to start by ordering true seeds rather than tubers. You shouldn't use just any old potato variety as a starting point for collecting true seed. Many commercial strains of potatoes (though the breeders will not say which ones for trade secret reasons) have beneficial characteristics, such as disease resistance, that have been imparted through crosses with wild potato varieties; these varieties have toxic properties that are reliably suppressed in the first-generation hybrids that are cloned for Certified Seed Potatoes, but they would **not** be reliably suppressed in the next generation grown from true seed. Growing random poisonous potatoes probably wouldn't be a big hit with the family.

In theory, if you have the facilities to measure solanine content, you could select the plants from that second generation whose tubers were nonpoisonous, pull the other plants, and ultimately create a variety that bred true without potential for poisonous potatoes. But in practice, it is a lot easier to stick with heirloom varieties provided as true seed.

There are very few sources for true potato seed that you can use to start. One unlikely but very productive place to get a small quantity of seed for research purposes is the USDA Germplasm Repository at http://www.ars-grin.gov/npgs/orders.html. Another source is New World Crops (www.newworldcrops.com). Some other sources can be found by using an Internet search engine, but these are mostly private individuals and seed savers.

Potatoes are an outbreeding plant, and as such you want to grow at least twenty potato plants to avoid inbreeding depression. Then, collect the berries from those plants that were the most resistant to diseases and pests, excluding berries from the runts or those that seemed particularly susceptible to problems. (Warning: when ripe, the berries smell appetizing but are poisonous to eat. Keep out of reach of children!) Put the berries in a blender with a cup of water, and process just enough at low speed to break up the berries and free the seed. Dump that into an open container to ferment for a couple of days, then pour off the water, rinse the seed, and let it dry for a few days on paper towels before dehydrating over a desiccant and store in a cool, dark place in a sealed container.

Within just a few years you will end up with your own strain of potatoes that grows optimally in your location and soil and that has also accumulated robust multiple-gene resistances to a variety of diseases and maybe even a pest or two.

Preparation and Preservation

Mature potatoes last longest in locations that are cool (42 to 50 degrees), dark, and humid with good ventilation. They should be checked weekly and any rotting potatoes removed before the rot spreads to other potatoes. In these conditions, the potatoes will remain sound and free of sprouts for up to 140 days; the specific time will vary with the particular potato. Commercial storage facilities with computer-controlled storage conditions can keep some potatoes as long as 210 days, but you are unlikely to create such perfect conditions at home.

New potatoes—those that have been harvested before the plant starts to die back and have not been sun cured—can't be stored this way as they go bad quickly. The alternative for both new and mature potatoes is freezing. To freeze potatoes, wash, dry, chop into slices or fries no more than one-quarter inch thick, water blanch for four minutes, cool in ice water for five minutes, pat dry, and then seal in freezer bags excluding as much air as possible.

Potatoes can also be dehydrated. Wash the potatoes, cut them into one-eighth–inch thick rounds, water blanch for eight minutes, cool in ice water for fifteen minutes, pat dry, and dehydrate according to the recommendations of the manufacturer of your dehydrator. The results can be stored in airtight jars for a year or more and, if you are ambitious, can be ground into a powder for making your own instant mashed potatoes.

Oven French Fries

Ingredients:

Nonstick cooking spray
Several large baking potatoes

Procedure:

Wash and dry the potatoes and preheat the oven to 450 degrees. Cut the potatoes into ¼-inch strips. Spray liberally with the nonstick cooking spray, season as desired, and place flat in a single layer on a nonstick baking sheet in the oven. Cook for 25 minutes, turning over after the first 10 minutes for even browning.

⊗ Oven french fries

16

Squash

Squash were cultivated more than 8,000 years ago in the Americas, and are now grown in almost endless variety in every region on the planet that supports agriculture. Their culinary uses extend from soups and salads to even pies, so their popularity is understandable.

In a culinary sense, squash are divided into two categories: summer squash (including zucchini, patty pan, and yellow) and winter squash (including acorn, Hubbard, butternut, spaghetti, pumpkins, and others). But in a botanical sense, squash are divided into four distinct species. Hubbard and buttercup squash are *Cucurbita maxima*; cushaw squash are *Cucurbita mixta*; butternut squash is *Cucurbita moschata*; and acorn squash, pumpkins, zucchini, and other summer squash are *Cucurbita pepo*.

All varieties of squash are rich in fiber, vitamin C, and carotenes that exert a protective influence against cancers. Winter squash also provide useful amounts of folic acid, omega-3 fatty acids, pantothenic acid, vitamin B1, vitamin B6, and niacin. With the exception of Hubbard squash (because the woody seed capsule is generally too tough), all squash seeds are edible. The seeds are high in minerals such as zinc, manganese, phosphorus, and iron, and studies have shown pumpkin seeds to reduce the symptoms of BPH (benign prostatic hyperplasia).

Variety Selection

The three most important things to consider in selecting varieties of squash to grow are the types of squash your family prefers to eat, the length of your growing season, and disease resistance. Most supermarkets carry a variety of winter squash year-round and summer squash seasonally. You can try various types to find out what you and your family prefer. Growing season is not generally a consideration for summer squash as they are harvested early, but some winter squash require a growing season well in excess of 100 days. The time to maturity for squash is measured from the time the seed is planted, so if you start your squash inside three weeks before planting out as a transplant, you can often squeeze a variety of squash into your season that otherwise wouldn't have enough time.

Powdery mildew is quite common in all varieties of squash and is the only disease for which a wide variety of resistant cultivars is available. If you have serious economic impact from powdery mildew, then consider growing squash varieties that are resistant.

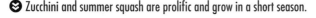 Zucchini and summer squash are prolific and grow in a short season.

Starting and Planting

In typical gardens, squash seeds are planted directly in hills or rows. However, both to maximize productivity in terms of season extension and to get a head start against pests or diseases, I recommend starting them indoors two weeks before last frost and putting out the transplants a week after last frost.

Optimum soil pH is between 6.5 and 6.8, though squash will grow satisfactorily at pH levels as low as 5.5 if the soil's fertility is otherwise optimal. Squash grow best with even soil moisture. Uneven moisture can cause blossom end rot and malformed fruit. As rain is unpredictable, the best way to assure the most even moisture uptake possible is to establish deep root systems and provide a great deal of organic matter in the soil. This can be accomplished by adding at least five cubic feet of compost per 4 ft. x 8 ft. bed so that the organic matter will buffer and hold moisture and through deep watering equivalent to one inch of rain at least once a week, but twice weekly in hot weather. Using raised beds will help to compensate for overwatering due to heavy rains by allowing excessive moisture to drain.

Squash require full sun, so the bed location should be optimally located for minimum shade. Some squash varieties, notably yellow, patty pan, and zucchini, grow on bushes. These varieties should be spaced at two-foot intervals throughout the bed. Others, such as acorn squash and pumpkins, grow a long vining system.

For smaller squash varieties, such as acorn squash, it is fine to put your transplants at one-foot intervals along the northern one foot of the bed and train the vines onto a trellis. But for larger squash varieties, such as Hubbard squash or large pumpkins, this isn't practical. The larger squash plants should be planted at one-foot intervals along the southern one foot of the bed and their vines allowed to grow across the yard. This way, the rest of the bed real estate can be used for another crop. You could grow small squash trellised along the northern foot of the bed, large squash along the southern foot of the bed, and a crop such as lettuce or chard in the two feet in between to make maximum use of space.

If the vines for larger squash are allowed to grow across the yard, you won't be able to control grass and weeds in that area, which could serve as a reservoir for pests and disease. To cut down on weeds and the pests/diseases they carry, that area can be heavily mulched with grass clippings, hay, or something similar.

Squash will also grow well planted in between cornstalks as long as you space the corn a bit wider than usual. It is also one of the very few plants that will do fine in companion plantings with onions.

Weeds, Pests, and Diseases

Weeds can sap nutrients, block sunlight, and give a safe haven to pests and diseases. Bush-type summer squash are planted far enough apart that a stirrup hoe, used shallowly once a week, can deal with the weeds. Weeding is likewise easy on smaller squash that are trellised, but the squash vines that are allowed to grow across the yard outside of the beds really need to be mulched under the vines to control weeds, as using a hoe or weeding by hand just isn't practical. Lots of materials can be used for mulch. I use grass clippings because they are free. Some studies indicate that using very shiny mulch, such as aluminum foil or Mylar, may help deter cucumber beetles; these should be placed on top of a regular mulch because all by themselves they won't hold back weeds.

The most common disease of squash is powdery mildew. This appears as a white or gray powdery-looking mold that results in deformed and dead leaves. It spreads rapidly and can wipe out a plant or even several plants within a few days of emerging. Prevention is better than attempting a cure, and the best preventatives are growing resistant varieties, planting in full sun, and avoiding nighttime watering. If the disease still takes hold, remove affected leaves and discard in the trash. (Make sure that the tools you use to cut off the leaves are disinfected after each cut by dipping in a 1:10 bleach solution before being used on other leaves or plants.) If that fails to halt the progress of the disease, try a milk and baking soda spray composed of one pint of milk and three teaspoons of baking soda for every

❄ Small winter squash can be trellised on the north side of a bed.

❄ As you can see, even larger winter squash grow fine on a trellis.

gallon of spray. Spray twice weekly, being sure to get both the tops and bottoms of the leaves.

Other important diseases of squash include bacterial wilt, anthracnose, angular leaf spot, and mosaic viruses. All of these diseases are either spread by pests that can be controlled, overwinter in the previous year's crop refuse, or both. So the most important preventative measures are crop rotation, cleaning up debris at the end of each season, and controlling pests.

Bacterial wilt is spread by cucumber beetles, and organic control is quite difficult, which is one reason organic squash varieties (pumpkins especially) from the U.S. are hard to find. Preventative measures include giving seedlings a head start through transplanting instead of sowing seed directly, covering the plants with floating row cover until the blossoms appear so they can produce at least some mature fruit before succumbing, planting trap crops that are more attractive than those being grown and that have been treated with a nonorganic insecticide, and using organic insecticides such as pyrethrin mixed with canola oil or diatomaceous earth prophylactically. In nonorganic gardens, carbaryl applied regularly according to package directions from the moment of seed emergence is effective.

Anthracnose fungus overwinters in crop debris and in seed collected from infected fruit. It usually starts as yellow spots on older leaves, but especially in warm, damp weather it can quickly spread to affect younger leaves, stems, and fruit. As the disease progresses, the spots get larger and turn brown, followed by the vine dying. Crop rotation and cleaning up the prior year's debris are the most important steps to prevent anthracnose. If your seed is of dubious origin, you can treat it with hot water as described in the chapter on peppers, but this will substantially reduce germination rates so start three times as many seedlings if you do this. Once anthracnose has made itself known, if you catch it early you can cut off and throw away infected leaves—this may prevent further spreading. Thereafter, spray neem oil according to package directions every seven to ten days as a preventative, making sure to get the undersides of leaves. Once the disease is clearly actively spreading, Soap Shield[1] copper fungicidal soap will control it if used quickly, as will Bordeaux mixtures of copper sulfate and lime.

Angular leaf spot overwinters in crop debris, so crop rotation and sanitation will effectively prevent it. Angular leaf spot gets its name from the spots it produces on leaves; they are confined to the leaf area between veins. The spots start as water-soaked spots that later turn brown and develop tears. It spreads like wild-

---

1   Soap Shield is a registered trademark of Gardens Alive, Inc.

fire in wet weather and is spread by people working with damp fruits, leaves, and vines. Prevention is better than cure, but if prevention fails, a copper fungicide will usually work if used soon after detection. Copper fungicides, used excessively, can harm soil biology and the runoff can harm fish. So, again, a concentration on prevention is wise.

Squash are affected by both squash mosaic and cucumber mosaic, transmitted by cucumber beetles and aphids, respectively. Cucumber beetle control has already been discussed in relation to bacterial wilt disease, and aphids can be controlled in a variety of ways. Insecticidal soap applied according to label directions is effective, as are the encapsulated natural pyrethrins. Garlic oil sprays will kill aphids, and most varieties of aphids can be deterred or killed with a tea made from potato or tomato leaves.

Squash (as well as cucumbers and melons to a lesser degree) are also affected by squash bugs. They suck the plant juices and inject a toxin that can weaken and kill the vines. Even worse, in four states (Oklahoma, Kentucky, Texas, and Ohio) they have been found to transmit Cucurbit Yellow Vine Disease. Squash bugs are about five-eighths inch long, dark brown or mottled with brown and gray, and hard-shelled. They are shield shaped and make a disagreeable odor when crushed. They lay their orange-yellow eggs in clusters of twelve or more on the underside of leaves. Adult squash bugs overwinter in crop debris, under mulches, and under boards. Avoiding mulches (other than hay, which seems to repel them) in beds that will be used for cucurbit family crops is a good idea, as is removal and composting of crop debris.

The best organic control of squash bugs is to cover the vines with floating row cover that is well anchored—so bugs can't sneak in—from the moment the crop is planted until the first flowers emerge. This will at least reduce the time frame available for them to do damage. You can try interplanting buckwheat to attract parasitic wasps that will prey on the squash bugs, but the results of this are marginal. Likewise, interplanting with marigolds or nasturtiums may have some marginal effect. On the scale of a mini farm, you can pick off the bugs and put them in some soapy water and smash the egg clusters by hand. If infestation can't be controlled that way, a pyrethrin/rotenone spray used according to label directions can control them.

The larvae of squash vine borers burrow into vines and destroy the tissue, thereby killing any part of the vine beyond where they entered. The adult is a moth whose coloration often leads to it being mistaken for a bee or wasp. It lays small blackish pinhead eggs, usually along the six inches of a vine just above where it emerges from the soil. When the eggs hatch, the larvae burrow into the vine,

« Squash bugs inject a poison into the vine.

growing as they eat until they are ultimately large enough that their burrowing physically disrupts the plant.

Squash vines will put roots into the soil anywhere the vine is covered with soil, so one thing that will help diminish the damage from borers is burying parts of the vine as it grows so that the vine has a diversified source of nutrients and water. Another thing you can try is wrapping some aluminum foil around the bottom six inches of the vine so the moth has no place to lay its eggs or has to settle for a less damaging place.

Observing your plants daily and particularly looking for "frass"—the sawdust-like leavings that borers leave behind them as they eat into the stems—can allow you to react before too much damage is done. If you catch it before the vine wilts, you can kill the borer in the vine by poking through it with a pin and leaving the pin in place. You can sometimes cut the stem along its length, extract the borer, push the vine back together where it was cut, and bury the cut section in soil.

Industrial agriculture depends on insecticides sprayed on a regular schedule to kill the larvae as they emerge from the eggs, but they are seldom a large enough problem on a mini farm to justify default use of insecticides "just in case."

Particularly in summer squash, blossom end rot is a possibility. As the name of the condition implies, the blossom end of the squash simply rots. This problem is caused by uneven uptake of calcium due to variations in water availability, such as two weeks without water followed by a sudden soaking rain. Often the first fruits of summer squash will have this problem, and it is nothing to worry about. Overall the problem can be prevented by making sure the beds have plenty of compost to buffer the water supply and watering regularly (once a week in normal weather but twice a week if it is hot and dry) and deeply to the equivalent of an inch of rain each time.

Harvest

Summer and winter squash are harvested differently. Summer squash are harvested while still immature, like cucumbers, so the plants will continue to make new flowers and squash. For the best flavor, yellow squash and zucchini should be harvested when no more than six inches to eight inches long, and patty pan squash should be harvested when no more than four inches in diameter. Once you allow a summer squash to mature, the plant stops making new ones, so make sure none escapes your notice, which can easily happen under the heavy cover provided by squash leaves. A couple of times I've missed squash that easily grew to several pounds. Not only did the plant stop making more squash, but the large squash was not very tasty.

Winter squash, on the other hand, are harvested when mature and they are cured for longer keeping. In fact, in most cases the flavor of winter squash varieties improves over the first several weeks after harvest. Winter squash are harvested when they have developed full color and their rinds are hard enough that they can't be dented with a thumbnail and the rind has become dull looking as opposed to glossy. Don't pull them off the vine, or their keeping quality will be adversely affected. Instead, cut the vine using pruners or a sharp knife, leaving two or three inches of vine still attached to the squash. With the exception of acorn types, other winter squash should then be cured by leaving them in the shade at temperatures exceeding 80 degrees for five to ten days before storing.

Seed Saving

The biggest challenge with seed saving is that squash require bees or other pollinators to pollinate, and interbreeding between varieties within the same species is quite easy. If you want to save seed, I would recommend growing only one type of squash of a given species each year.

Cucurbita pepo: Yellow, zucchini, patty pan, acorn, spaghetti, and common pumpkin

Cucurbita moschata: butternut, Naples, Kentucky field pumpkin, neck pumpkin

Cucurbita mixta: cushaw squash (looks like a pumpkin)

Cucurbita maxima: buttercup, Hubbard, banana, Lakota

Squash flowers are very attractive to bees and rely on them for pollination. »

There is room for confusion, particularly with squash known as pumpkins, because there are many varieties of pumpkins and the term encompasses squash from more than one species. Just to be on the safe side, when ordering seeds for squash, check the catalog to make sure what species it is.

Winter squash used for seeds should be taken three or even four weeks later than the squash would normally be harvested. Also, those squash that grow closest to the root of the plant are likely to produce seeds with the highest rate of germination. Scoop out the seeds, swirl them around in a bowl of lukewarm water, dry off with some paper towels, and allow them to sit for a couple of weeks before drying further over a desiccant. Store in an airtight container in a cool, dark place.

Summer squash are treated identically. If you leave them long enough, they will get large and grow a tough rind. Once this rind is tough enough, you can't dent it with your thumbnail. Let the squash mature for another three weeks before harvesting.

Preparation and Preservation

Summer squash can be kept in a plastic bag in the crisper drawer of your refrigerator, but it will only keep for three to five days. Like sweet corn, it is one of those vegetables best eaten or preserved soon after harvest. The best way to preserve summer squash is freezing. Cut off the ends, slice uniformly, water blanch for three minutes or steam blanch for five minutes, cool in ice water for five minutes, pat dry, and then store in freezer bags with as much air excluded as possible.

Winter squash should be stored at a temperature of 50–55 degrees. Acorn type squash will keep for one or two months, butternut, turban, and butternut squash will keep for two or three months, and Hubbard squash for as long as six months. Storage life can be enhanced even longer if, after the fruits have been cured and before you store them, you wash the surface using a cloth dipped in soapy water (dish liquid is fine) that contains one part bleach for every ten parts of soapy water. This kills many of the pathogens that would normally affect the squash, thus prolonging storage life. Check your stored squash frequently and discard those showing signs of rotting promptly so spoors don't spread to adjacent fruit. The optimal humidity for storage is 50 percent to 70 percent. Higher than that will decrease storage life due to increased rotting, and lower than that will decrease storage life due to dehydration of the fruit. Don't store winter squash near apples as the ethylene gas that apples generate will cause the squash to rot.

The seeds of any edible squash (including pumpkins) can be eaten (though those of the largest varieties may be too tough), and they make a tasty high-energy snack. There are several ways to prepare them depending upon one's preferences and health-consciousness. To preserve the healthful character of the oils in squash seeds, they shouldn't be cooked at a temperature higher than 170 degrees. On the other hand, cooking at higher temperatures is preferred by many because it results in a different taste. Seeds prepared either way will keep for a week if stored in an airtight container in the refrigerator.

To prepare in this fashion, clean the seeds by swishing them around in a big bowl of warm water, then strain them out of the water and dry them on paper towels overnight. Preheat your oven to 160–170 degrees, and spread the seeds in a single layer on a baking sheet. Bake for twenty minutes, use a spatula to flip the seeds, and then bake for another ten minutes.

To go all-out on snack food, clean the seeds as above, preheat the oven to 450 degrees, mix the seeds in a large bowl with canola oil and a bit of Adobo,[2] and then

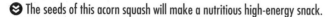

The seeds of this acorn squash will make a nutritious high-energy snack.

---

2   "Adobo" in this case is a seasoning available in the Latin section of the supermarket. I use the Adobo con Cumin for this recipe.

put in a single layer on the baking sheet. Cook for ten minutes, flip with a spatula, and then cook for another ten minutes.

Baked Acorn Squash

Ingredients:

2 acorn squash (will also work with butternut, buttercup, delicata, etc.)
4 tbsp butter
¼ cup packed brown sugar
salt and pepper to taste

Procedure:

Preheat oven to 400 degrees. Cut the squash in half lengthwise and remove the seeds. Cook the halves in a shallow pan with the cut side down for thirty minutes. Turn them with the cut side up, then add the butter, sugar, salt and pepper. Return to the oven and cook for another 30-40 minutes until a fork can be easily inserted.

Summer Squash Casserole

Ingredients:

2 lbs summer squash (yellow, zucchini, patty pan, or any combination)
1 beaten egg
2 cups chopped tomatoes
1 onion, chopped
1 cup bread crumbs
2 tbsp melted butter
½ tsp salt

Procedure:

Preheat the oven to 350 degrees. Slice the squash and cook in a bowl in the microwave for 5 minutes, stopping to stir at the halfway point. Thoroughly combine the bread crumbs, salt, beaten egg, and tomatoes and salt thoroughly, then stir in the squash. Use the butter to grease a casserole dish. Dump all the ingredients into the casserole dish and bake for 45 minutes.

17

Tomatoes

If there is any one thing that motivates more people to take up gardening, it is the desire to eat a tomato right off the vine. The tomatoes in the supermarket usually look perfect, but they taste unripe and have little flavor. Many people remember the taste of tomatoes right out of their mother's or grandfather's garden, and they know they don't have to settle for the unappetizing fare at the store.

Not only are tomatoes a nutritional powerhouse rich in vitamins A and C along with various minerals and B vitamins, but study after study has shown that a diet rich in tomatoes is protective against a variety of cancers, including prostate and pancreatic cancer. Other studies have shown that important antioxidants in tomatoes, such as lycopene, are present in greater quantities when the tomatoes are raised organically, so growing your own would be a tremendous benefit in more than just taste.

One thing you may find helpful in your quest for higher levels of self-sufficiency is how easy it is to make your own spaghetti sauce, salsa, and even ketchup from your own tomatoes.

Variety Selection

There are literally hundreds of different varieties of tomatoes encompassing colors from yellow to purple, as well as variations in growing habits, disease resistance, early or late maturities, and a range of flavors that makes tomatoes the subject of tastings similar to wine. There is no way to even make a dent in all the varieties available, but there are a number of ways to make sense of them.

Tomatoes are either determinate, meaning bush-like, or indeterminate, meaning vine-like. Determinate varieties can be grown using just a short tomato cage, but indeterminate varieties will need a trellis to maximize their potential. Determinate tomatoes also tend to ripen more closely together, whereas the tomatoes on indeterminate vines will ripen at different times. For purposes of processing large numbers of tomatoes for spaghetti sauce or ketchup, determinate varieties are usually best, but for adding to salads throughout the summer or for drying in batches, you might find indeterminate varieties more convenient.

The maturity date for tomatoes listed in seed catalogs is based on the number of days since they were put in the garden as transplants. Usually, you will want tomatoes for both early in the season and later in the season, so you might grow a couple of varieties to have your harvest spread out.

Though in most respects tomatoes can be readily substituted for each other, there are differences in moisture content that make some tomatoes more suitable for sauces and other more suitable for fresh eating. For example, the Italian plum varieties tend to have a lower moisture content, so they don't have to be simmered as long to make a thick sauce.

Tomatoes come in a variety of colors ranging from white to purple. There are even varieties that remain green when ripe! In general, the tomatoes rated most highly in taste tests are pink, purple, or black varieties. (These latter aren't really black. They have a complex darker color.) Examples include Pruden's Purple and Brandywine. However, only your taste and opinion matter.

In my garden, I usually grow an indeterminate cherry tomato for salad tomatoes all season, an early slicer for sandwiches and a late slicer for even more sandwiches, and a group of determinate paste tomatoes for sauce and salsa. I like Peacevine cherry for salads; Moskvich and Stupice for early season slicing; Brandywine and Pruden's Purple for late season slicing; and Amish Paste, Black Plum, and Plum for sauces among others. But those are just my own preferences.

Starting and Planting

Tomatoes are a warm weather crop and, as long as they are supplied with sufficient water, the more sun and heat the better. This makes tomatoes a bit of a challenge for northern growers, but breeders have put a great deal of effort into producing early tomatoes, especially in Eastern Europe. So with proper variety selection, tomatoes certainly belong in gardens across the continental United States.

If you've ever had tomatoes rot in the garden and been faced with dozens if not hundreds of volunteer plants the following year, you know that tomatoes can be directly seeded in the garden. Volunteers need to be ruthlessly culled because they can serve as a reservoir of disease (for both tomatoes and potatoes) that negates the value of crop rotation. Even so, putting seeds in the ground directly is not very reliable and in most parts of the country, tomatoes could definitely benefit from a head start. Maturity dates given for tomatoes in catalogs assume the use of transplants started six weeks earlier, so a bit of math shows that sowing them directly from seed won't allow for enough time before frost sets in in the fall in most of the country. Start them indoors six weeks before last frost, and plant them out right after the last expected frost.

If you are growing indeterminate tomatoes, plant them spaced eighteen inches apart in the northern one foot of the bed and train them onto a trellis six feet tall. Prune the tops back once they reach that high. If you are growing determinate tomatoes, use the cheap wire tomato cages and space them eighteen inches to twenty-four inches apart. Ideally, these will be in a bed that has the long sides on the east and west so the tomatoes will benefit from sun on both sides of the bed.

The soil for tomatoes should be deeply worked, incorporating a lot of organic matter. I would recommend at least five cubic feet of compost per 4 ft. x 8 ft. bed. The pH should ideally be in the 6.5 to 7 range, though closer to 6.5 is better for prevention of a condition known as yellow shoulder. Uneven uptake of calcium due to uneven uptake of water causes blossom end rot and splitting in tomatoes. The organic matter will help hold and buffer the water while using a raised bed will help prevent an overabundance.

Too much nitrogen can cause tomato plants to create lots of foliage but bland tomatoes. So when you add amendments in accordance with a soil test, use slow-release nitrogen sources such as alfalfa meal, cottonseed meal, and compost as opposed to sodium nitrate, urea, or blood meal, and don't add any more than the soil testing indicates. If you mix a tablespoon of garden gypsum into the soil of the hole where you plant tomatoes, it will also help prevent blossom end rot.

Tomatoes will send down roots anywhere the stem is covered with soil. For the most robust root system and plants, put the tomatoes deep in the soil with the stem horizontal and only four inches of the plant above ground. As the plant grows, strip off the leaves that are within a foot of the ground, as this step will help prevent a variety of blights and other diseases that start with infecting the lower leaves.

Weeds, Pests, and Diseases

Because tomatoes are planted with such wide spacing, controlling weeds via careful periodic hoeing is straightforward, and the foliage is often so plentiful at close spacing that much weed competition is shaded out once the plants are growing well.

Because tomato foliage is poisonous to most things, tomatoes only have a few notable pests; among these are hornworms, cutworms, flea beetles, aphids, white-flies, and root-knot nematodes.

Aphids will always exist to some degree on tomato plants and they don't usually pose a problem, but if their numbers become too large they can weaken the plants. They can be controlled with a couple sprays of insecticidal soap. Cutworms will exist in any bed that has had fresh organic matter (such as cover crops or heavy weeds) cut and turned into the bed within a couple of weeks of planting. Protect the seedlings with cardboard collars four inches long and buried an inch

deep in the soil when they are first planted, and you'll have no trouble.

Tomato hornworms are such a unique creature that once you've seen one, you'll never forget it. They have a

❰❰ Lay the stem horizontally when transplanting for maximum-strength roots.

prominent horn at one end, are as long as three inches, and are green with stripes and eye-like markings over their body. They gobble foliage extensively, even chopping off entire branches of the plant at times. You can pick these off and feed them to the chickens. I've never found more than a few of these in a single season, but if your plants are suffering from an extensive infestation, they can be controlled overnight with a single complete spraying with a *Bacillus thuringiensis* preparation used according to label directions.

Whiteflies are not usually a problem when using homegrown transplants; they often hitchhike on plants purchased from nurseries or garden stores. In small quantities, these don't adversely affect the plant. In large populations they can leave a lot of honeydew on the plant that gives room for sooty mold to take hold. Sooty mold looks like a sooty coating on leaves and fruits. It doesn't actually infect the plant but rather lives in the honeydew on the surface. It isn't economically important unless it becomes so extensive as to block sunlight and photosynthesis. Whiteflies are ubiquitous in garden stores, greenhouses, and the like because over the decades they have become immune to practically all insecticides. If you develop a substantial infestation of whiteflies, about the only thing that will control them is a light horticultural oil. Don't use such oils during a drought or they can kill the plant.

⊗ Tomato hornworms have a unique beauty, but they are voracious.

Flea beetles resemble fleas. A few of them won't hurt anything, but if the populations are high, they can defoliate and weaken the plants. If their damage crosses an economic threshold, they can be easily controlled with a pyrethrin/rotenone spray used according to package directions.

Perhaps the most dreaded pest of tomatoes is root-knot nematodes. These microscopic worms burrow into the roots causing knots that interfere with nutrient absorption and the full cycle of photosynthesis. The preparations used to control them on a commercial scale are breathtakingly toxic and expensive and thus impractical on a mini farm; they are better off prevented. Luckily, they can be prevented easily through crop rotation and sanitation. At the end of the season, pull out all plants, including as much of the roots as you can, and compost them. If you develop an infestation in a bed, I would recommend growing mustard in that bed for a couple of years, followed by onions the next year. Then try a crop such as beets that is susceptible to root knot nematodes and where the damage will easily be seen to find out if you've successfully abolished them. If not, go back to the mustard and onions for another couple of years.

A common but seldom recognized pest of tomatoes is the tomato russet mite. The symptoms start with the lower leaves turning brown and then move up the plant with the stem taking on a bronze-like appearance. If they appear, you can control tomato russet mites with a commercial wettable sulfur preparation.

Diseases of tomatoes include fusarium wilt, verticillium wilt, and mosaic viruses, among others, though tomatoes can also be affected by potato early and late blight, manifesting identical symptoms to potatoes. The key to controlling diseases is crop rotation and sanitation. Only once have I ever had a problem with disease in tomatoes, and those seedlings were brought home from a nursery (purchased after an unexpected late and hard frost killed our seedlings). Otherwise, by following the simple precautions of rotation, sanitation, and keeping tobacco products away from the plants, I've never had a problem.

Fusarium wilt affects all nightshade family plants including tomatoes, eggplant, peppers, and potatoes. Fusarium usually times its arrival for damp weather when there is already lots of full-sized green fruit on the plant, turning the leaves yellow. There seems to be no rhyme or reason to which leaves will be affected, and sometimes it will infect one half of the leaves but not the other. Those leaves lose the power of photosynthesis, and the fruit doesn't get enough energy to ripen. Fusarium is a soil-born fungus that can be controlled by crop rotation. If problems persist, there are many varieties of tomatoes that are resistant, so if you choose a resistant variety it won't be an issue.

Verticillium wilt usually starts on the older leaves with the edges turning first yellow then brown. Unlike fusarium, it doesn't kill the plant, but it definitely hurts productivity. Crop rotation and sanitation are your biggest preventatives, as the pathogen is soil-born. I have found another solution. What I do is sow my tomato bed in clover, and grow indeterminate varieties trellised on the north side of the bed. The clover creates a dense ground cover that keeps rain from splattering fungus spoors from the soil up onto the leaves. I plant the transplants in the clover patch, take off the bottom leaves once they get big enough, and train them onto a trellis. For determinate plants where trellising isn't feasible, they tend to shade out the clover so the protection isn't as full, but a number of verticillium-resistant varieties of tomato are also available.

There are many mosaic viruses, but they all have the same symptoms on tomatoes. The leaves develop a mottled appearance, wilt, and grow small—almost like a fern. The result is a plant that fails to thrive. Plants infected with such viruses should be discarded in the rubbish.

Now for the good news: your tomatoes will never suffer from this virus. The reason is because 99.9 percent of the time, mosaic virus comes from tobacco in cigarettes when the gardener fails to wash his or her hands after smoking and then transmits the virus to the tomatoes. If you smoke, all you need to do is avoid smoking in or around your garden and wash your hands after smoking before touching tomato (or potato or pepper) plants, and you will never see this virus.

Pinching and Pruning Tomatoes

As mentioned earlier, tomatoes can be divided into determinate and indeterminate types. Determinate plants only reach a certain size and do not require extensive pruning or a trellis; indeterminate plants, given proper conditions, will literally grow with no limits. Determinate plants only need a cage or a stake—though I much prefer cages. Indeterminate plants will grow adjunct stems at leaf axils in an infinite variety and, if left unchecked, will outgrow practically any trellis and start creeping along the ground.

Because of soil-borne diseases, it is important to keep tomatoes off the ground. Thus cages for determinate tomatoes and trellising for indeterminate tomatoes are absolutely necessary. Pruning indeterminate tomatoes is an exercise in discretion; understanding why it is needed will help put it in context.

The more vegetative growth a tomato plant produces, the more of that growth will be shaded thus consuming more sugar than it produces. Furthermore, the

Excess stems can be easily pinched off when they are small.

more vegetation, the more fruit clusters, the smaller the fruit, and the later it will ripen. Too much vegetation will also favor disease conditions due to the prolonged time required for moisture to evaporate from the leaves. There is an optimal trade-off between the number of stems and the size, and the number and speed of maturation of fruits. In most cases, this is just three or at most four adjunct stems.

How high up on the plant these stems grow is important. You don't want them growing from below the first fruit cluster because they will put too much strain on the root. You don't want them growing too high on the plant because then they will be too weak to support fruits of their own. What I recommend is allowing a new stem to grow from the leaf axils immediately above the first, second, and third fruit clusters; and ruthlessly pinching off any others.

In between the leaves and the stems (an area known as the axil) is where the new stems emerge. Once you see it growing small leaves, you'll know it is a new stem. These new stems are most easily removed by "pinching." Just grasp between your thumb and forefinger and literally pinch it off. This method exposes the least amount of remaining tissue to disease. Sometimes, though, the plants get away from you and you'll have a stem three feet long before you realize it; such stems that can't be removed by pinching should be removed with the least tissue damage possible by using a razor knife in preference to tools such as scissors or pruners.

Indeterminate tomatoes should also be "topped." About a month before your first expected frost, you want to cut the top off of any growing stems. This will force all energy production to go into ripening the fruit.

Because damp conditions favor the spread of disease, never prune tomatoes when the plants are damp. And because diseases spread easily between plants, I recommend dipping any tools used in a 10% bleach/water solution after each cut.

Harvest

Tomatoes can be eaten at any time and size. Though green tomatoes contain small amounts of the poisonous alkaloid tomatine, no cases of poisoning have been reported from their consumption and studies indicate that the tomatine binds to cholesterol in the digestive tract, preventing absorption of both the tomatine and the cholesterol. In the concentrations present in green tomatoes, consumption has been shown to lower bad LDL cholesterol, inhibit certain cancers, and enhance immune response.[1] So green tomatoes are safe to harvest and eat.

Even so, I much prefer my tomatoes ripe—especially for fresh eating—and I suspect most folks share my preference. Vine-ripened fruits are by far the most tasty, with those ripening indoors rating a very close second.

Timing the harvest is straightforward: pick the tomato when it has developed maximum color for its variety but has not become soft. There are two exceptions to this rule. The first is cherry tomatoes because of their tendency to split. Harvest these when the color has changed but before maximum ripeness to avoid splitting. The second is any variety of tomato that is prone to cracking. These should also be harvested before maximum color.

Problems with cracking can occur in any tomato that has been water-deprived for an extended period of time and then given an overabundance of water. Incorporating plenty of organic matter into the soil as a buffer to absorb and release water as needed will be helpful, as will growing in raised beds and making sure tomatoes are watered properly. But even with the best care, some varieties are prone to splitting as ripeness approaches, and these should be harvested before they crack.

Tomatoes harvested a little early will continue to ripen indoors. Ideally, put them in a closed paper bag at room temperature. A paper bag will retain and concentrate ripening factors such as the ethylene gas released by the ripening fruit that also triggers further ripening, but it will also keep the fruit from becoming water-laden and rotten as would happen with a plastic bag. You can hasten the ripening process by putting a ripe (but not overripe) banana in the bag with the tomatoes.

If you know a frost is coming and you have a lot of green fruits on your plants, you can either harvest the green fruits and use them in appropriate recipes or cut

---

1   McGee, H. (2009), "Accused but Probably not a Killer," *New York Times*, July 18, 2009, ISSN 0362-4331

the vines and hang them upside down indoors in the dark. Surprisingly, a lot of the fruit will ripen.

Seed Saving

Tomatoes usually self-pollinate. That is, the pollen fertilizes the ovum within the flower, sometimes before the flower even opens. To help this process, you can give your tomato plants a little shake now and then. Even though tomatoes are self-pollinating, they can also be cross-pollinated by insects, so maintain several feet of separation between plants of different varieties from which you want to save seeds. Also, use only open-pollinated or heirloom varieties for seed saving as hybrids will not make seed that re-creates the characteristics of the immediate parent.

When you save tomato seeds, you want to save them from the very best tomatoes on the very best plants. Pick the tomato slightly before it is fully ripe. If you wait until it is fully ripe, it will hurt the germination rates of the seeds you save. Tomato seeds are processed using a fermentation method.

Cut the tomato across the equator, and use your clean fingers or a spoon to scoop the gelatin and seeds (but not the meat of the tomato) into a clean container. I use small plastic cups, but canning jars will also work fine. Add water equivalent to about half the volume of tomato gelatin in the cups, and swirl it around with a spoon. Cover the top with cheesecloth to keep out bugs, and set aside for two to four days until a mold starts growing on top. If four days have elapsed and there is still no mold, don't worry. Add water to the cups, swish it around, and pour off any mold or floating seeds. Rinse off with water a few times, and then spread the seeds on multiple layers of paper towels to dry. After about a week, put the seeds on a paper plate to dry further. After another week, you can dry further over a desiccant before storing for up to four years in a sealed container in a cool, dry, dark place.

Preparation and Preservation

If you wash and dry your tomatoes when you bring them in, they'll keep for a week without loss of flavor just sitting on the kitchen counter and longer if they are not yet ripe. They will keep for yet another week in the refrigerator, but at the cost of some loss of flavor and a sort of graininess being imparted to the flesh. Between the two methods, you can save up your tomatoes for a couple of weeks (if you are saving for a batch of sauce).

Tomatoes can also be dehydrated, canned, and even frozen. Though vegetables are usually blanched before dehydrating and freezing, this is not needed with tomatoes, though many prefer to remove the skin and the procedure for doing so tends to blanch them a bit anyway.

Many recipes call for removing the skin from the tomatoes because, especially when canned, the skin can become tough and a detracting annoyance in some dishes. Once you get the hang of removing the skin, it is easy. Bring some water in a pot to a gentle boil. Make sure it is deep enough to fully cover the tomato. Lower the tomato into the water on a slotted metal spoon. Leave it in the water until the skin starts cracking—about a minute—and then put the tomato in ice water for three minutes. The skin is then easily removed. Once the skin is removed, you can also remove the hard core from the tomato by using a simple apple corer. Once the tomato has been skinned and cored, you can cut it, remove the gelatinous portion containing the seeds, and either freeze directly in a freezer bag from which air has been excluded or dehydrate according to the directions that came with your dehydrator.

For making sauces, I don't bother with removing seeds, skins, or cores. Instead, I boil up the tomatoes in a big pot until they are mushy and then process them through a hand-cranked strainer that separates out these portions.

Canning tomatoes is a borderline proposition; that is, the pH of tomato is right on the borderline between foods that can be safely canned in a water bath and foods that require pressure canning. Most recipes in canning books specify the addition of an acidifying substance—usually commercial bottled lemon juice—as a means of lowering the pH sufficiently to allow for safe water bath canning. The reason they specify commercially bottled lemon juice is because it contains a predictable and standardized amount of citric acid. The problem is that the stuff usually contains potassium sorbate as a preservative. Even though as far as I know potassium sorbate is not harmful, it has been my experience that when used in products that are cooked, it imparts off flavors. So instead I recommend that you go on the Internet to any wine-making hobby store and order pure citric acid. Substitute one-quarter teaspoon of citric acid for one tablespoon of lemon juice, and you will achieve the same effect without imparting unintended off flavors. Also, keep in mind that if you add any other vegetable or meat to a tomato recipe (except salsa because salsa is actually a pickle), you will need to pressure can that product for the longest length of time for any of the ingredients. Failure to do so can result in botulism.

There are a host of recipes for relishes, salsas, chutneys, and pies (for the adventurous) made from green tomatoes. Some like to slice them, dip them in egg and then seasoned flour, and fry them. All of these recipes are wonderful.

Homemade Ketchup
Ingredients:

20–25 lbs tomatoes

3 cups vinegar

1 cup chopped onions

1 cup chopped sweet red pepper

1 cup sugar

1 clove garlic

2 tsp celery seed

A strainer comes in handy for making large batches of sauce and ketchup for canning.

1 tsp salt
1 tsp whole black pepper
2 tsp whole allspice
2 tsp mustard seed
1 stick of cinnamon
½ tsp cayenne pepper

Procedure:

Clean and weigh the tomatoes. I use a kitchen scale, but for this quantity of produce you can use the bathroom scale. Cut them up whole and put them in a large pot with a little water to prevent scorching. Add the onions, garlic, sweet peppers, celery seed, salt, and cayenne pepper, cooking them over medium-low heat until they are mushy. While you are waiting on that, put the black pepper, allspice, mustard seed, and cinnamon in a spice bag. Bring the 3 cups of vinegar to a simmer in a smaller pot, put the spice bag in the vinegar, and allow that to simmer for 20–30 minutes. Remove the spice bag and turn off the heat on that burner.

Once the tomatoes and other ingredients in the pot are mushy, carefully process them through a hand-cranked strainer. Clean out the pot, dry it, and then put the liquid that results from the straining back into the pot. Add the vinegar and sugar. Bring to a simmer for 30 minutes.

After this, you need to either let it simmer while stirring for about 12 hours to get rid of the liquid, or put it in a large crock pot. I recommend the crock pot. Once the ketchup has simmered for about 12 hours and become thicker, fill sterilized pint jars leaving one-quarter inch of headspace and process in a boiling water canner for 30 minutes.

Allow this to set for a couple of weeks before use for full flavor to develop. You'll be amazed at how good this is!

18

Turnips, Rutabagas, and Radishes

Some variants of turnips, rutabagas, and radishes have been cultivated for hundreds and even thousands of years for good reason: they are versatile, nutritious, and delicious! Both the roots and leaves of all three are edible and can be cooked in a variety of ways. All three roots are high in vitamin C, folate, thiamine, niacin, and a number of essential minerals including potassium and copper. Their omega-3 to omega-6 fat ratio is 3:1, and they are a substantial source of cardio-protective dietary fiber.

But the good news continues into the leaves of these staple crops. The greens are strongly anti-inflammatory, and a single serving contains 350 percent of the RDA of vitamin A along with a whopping 1,050 percent of the RDA of vitamin K, a quarter of the day's supply of vitamin E and calcium, along with valuable quantities of folate, copper, manganese, and more. In essence, just like their closely related cousins broccoli and cabbage, turnips, rutabagas, and radishes are superfoods.

Turnips were a staple crop for settling the American West because they keep well in root cellars while supplying vital vitamin C throughout the harsh winters. Turnips, and turnip greens in particular, tend to be more appreciated in the American South than in the rest of the country, but their taste and nutritional properties argue in favor of a place in the garden.

Eaten raw, a small slice of turnip, rutabaga, or radish will share a characteristic pungency from the allyl isothiocyanate created by damage to the cells. These isothiocyanate compounds are a defense mechanism to keep herbivores from eating the plants, but in the small quantities normally consumed in food, they are perfectly safe. Even better, these isothiocyanates and related compounds induce the production of what are called "phase 2 detoxification enzymes" in the liver that selectively detoxify carcinogens.[1, 2] Cooking tends to remove the bite by eliminating an enzymatic precursor to isothiocyanate formation, but studies indicate that this doesn't adversely affect the formation of detoxification enzymes.[3]

All of this means that turnips, rutabagas, and radishes are potent cancer preventatives, and if your turnips have a sharp taste when raw, that just means they are good for you.

Variety Selection

Your local agricultural store likely only carries two varieties of turnip at most: Purple Top White Globe and Golden Ball. But if you look in the catalogs of heirloom seed companies, you'll find at least a dozen varieties from which to choose. As there are no particular diseases for which resistant varieties exist, your primary selection criteria is your own interests and tastes.

This same applies to rutabagas. At the agricultural store you'll be lucky to find even one variety, but you'll find at least half a dozen varieties in heirloom seed

---

1   Keum YS, Jeong WS & Kong AN (2004) "Chemoprevention by isothiocyanates and their underlying molecular signaling mechanisms." *Mutat Res* 555, 191–202.

2   Zhang YS, Yao S & Li J (2006) "Vegetable-derived isothiocyanates: anti-proliferative activity and mechanism of action." *Proc Nutr Soc* 65, 68–75.

3   Rungapamestry, V., Rabot, S., Fuller, Z., Ratcliffe, B., Duncan, A. (2008) "Influence of cooking duration of cabbage and presence of colonic microbiota on the excretion of N-acetylcysteine conjugates of allyl isothiocyanate and bioactivity of phase 2 enzymes in F344 rats." *British Journal of Nutrition* (2008), 99, 773–781

Seeds for Purple Top turnips are readily available and they produce reliably. ⊗

catalogs. Rutabagas are sweeter than turnips, and if your family hasn't developed a taste yet for this family of root vegetables, rutabagas would be a good place to start. Just look through the catalogs and find a variety that looks tasty.

Radishes are an entirely different proposition! With at least three dozen readily available varieties ranging from white to red to black and ranging in size from the size of your thumb to the size of an apple, you will find a lot of offerings that look nothing at all like the vegetable you associate with the word "radish." Initially, I would recommend trying a very common variety that looks familiar, such as French Breakfast. After that, though, you should branch out to try many different varieties.

Starting and Planting

Turnips, rutabagas, and radishes are grown from seed placed directly in the ground. Being brassicas, they are somewhat cold-hardy and can be planted anytime the average soil temperature is 50 degrees or higher, but it is best to wait for a soil temperature of 55 for best germination. They will sprout in from one to five days depending on soil temperature. The seeds should be planted one-half inch deep. When planting turnips and rutabagas, the best technique for maximizing harvest is to space at three inches in all directions, and then come back in about forty-five days to harvest every other plant for greens and young roots. Leave the others to grow larger. Radishes can be spaced at two-inch intervals, though some varieties can grow as large as turnips, so you should check the seed packet for the final thinning distance for the particular variety you are planting.

As with all root crops, deeply dug soil free of rocks will encourage the best growth. Plenty of finished compost (at least two cubic feet per 32 sq. ft. bed) will encourage the proper biological environment. It is important that the compost be finished, however, as turnips, rutabagas, and radishes are especially sensitive to the germination inhibitors present in unfinished compost. Maintaining a soil pH between 6 and 7 is optimal for these plants. The soil should have plenty of trace minerals either from a wide variety of additives of biological origin or supplemented with sea solids. Boron is a key element for proper growth. Boron is contained in borax and constitutes 11.5 percent of its weight. You need 300–400 milligrams of boron per 32 sq. ft. bed; 1½ teaspoons of borax will supply just the right amount. (Use a real measuring spoon; don't "eyeball" it.) Borax is toxic to plants in concentrated form, so you should mix it thoroughly with some other powdery additive, such as greensand or wood ashes, and distribute evenly. The macronutrients should be supplemented as indicated by a soil test.

A higher quality crop with fewer pest problems can be assured by planting for a fall harvest. That is because once temperatures exceed 75 degrees and most certainly when you get 90 degree days, the quality of the roots suffers dramatically. Rutabagas shrink and become stringy, radishes become woody, and turnips become just plain unpalatable. Rutabagas and turnips require sixty to ninety days to reach harvesting size. Even when planting six weeks before last frost in the spring, you are in a race against hot weather on the one end while combating root maggots on the other. If, instead, you plant six weeks before your first expected frost, you will get rapid germination, the season for cabbage maggots will be past, and the roots will be maturing during cooler days. You'll appreciate the results.

Radishes mature much more quickly, sometimes in as little as three weeks. So these are a lot easier to plant as a reliable spring crop because you can have them planted and harvested before warm weather.

Weeds, Pests, and Diseases

Because of their rapid germination and prolific growth, if planted in a weed-free bed initially, weeds are unlikely to be an issue. What little weeding is required can be done by hand and will mostly be at the outside edges of the beds where the weeds can get light.

Turnips, rutabagas, and radishes have good natural protection from predation and generally do not experience problems of economic importance on the scale of a mini farm, so long as crop rotation and sanitation are practiced.

The only economically serious disease that is likely is clubroot, a disease that results in stunted roots unable to draw water so the plants wilt and die. This can be avoided by keeping the soil pH above 6 and preferably 6.5. Once clubroot is in the soil of a bed, you can't grow any cabbage family crops there for eight years, so it pays to do a pH test and adjust the pH if needed so this disease doesn't gain a foothold.

Most pests aren't keen on the peppery taste of these plants, but anything that affects broccoli or cabbage can theoretically come after your turnips if sufficiently hungry. If they do, just treat as described in the chapter on cabbage and broccoli. The only pest I have seen in turnips that poses a substantive threat—and it is completely preventable—is cabbage root maggots. Cabbage root maggots are the larvae of a fly that looks like a slightly smaller and more streamlined version of a housefly. They overwinter as pupae in the soil, and emerge at the time you'd usually plant seeds. Once the plants emerge, they lay eggs at the base of the plant that burrow into the soil and then eat the roots voraciously. With root vegetables, you may not even know they have been affected until a very disappointing harvest.

Two factors disproportionately attract this pest. The first is rotting organic matter in the soil, such as immature compost. The second is planting when the soil temperature is a little too cold. If you avoid immature compost, plant at an average soil temperature of 55 degrees, and make sure you don't plant where cabbage family crops were grown last year, this pest can be completely prevented by covering your bed with floating row cover once the seeds are planted. Remove the row cover once soil temperatures average 65 degrees, and you are home free.

Harvest

You don't want turnips, rutabagas, or radishes to wait too long in the ground as they'll get woody and their flavor will suffer. Once soil temperatures are averaging above 75 degrees, they need to be harvested even if they are smaller than you'd like. Turnips for "bunching" —to be sold with greens and root together— should be harvested at a diameter of two inches. Those that will be "topped,"— meaning that the roots will be sold or used without the greens, should be harvested at a diameter of three inches. If you are like me, you have seen so-called "turnips" in the produce aisle at the grocery store that are a solid five or six inches in diameter. These aren't turnips—they are rutabagas. Rutabagas should be harvested at four inches for optimum quality. The reason they are so large in the supermarket is because they sell on the basis of weight rather than quality.

Radishes can be harvested at practically any stage, so long as you don't let them wait more than a week or so after they have reached the mature size for the variety you are growing. After that, they tend to split and become less tasty.

Seed Saving

Turnips, rutabagas, and radishes are biennials that produce flowers and seed in their second year. Turnips and radishes are outbreeding plants subject to inbreeding depression if too few are grown for seed and depend upon pollinators such as bees for pollination as they don't usually self-pollinate. Rutabagas are self-fertile and naturally inbreeding, though they will outbreed with the help of bees.

Radishes won't interbreed with other cabbage family crops with the exception of other radishes. So only grow one variety of radishes for seed in any given year. Grow at least twelve plants for seed.

Turnips will interbreed with other turnips, broccoli rabe, and Chinese cabbages. Only grow one variety of turnip (and no Chinese cabbage or broccoli rabe) for seed in a season. You should grow at least six plants for seed, but I would recommend an even dozen.

Rutabagas will interbreed with other rutabagas and with some varieties of turnip that are grown as livestock feed. Rape (a relative of mustard) can also interbreed with rutabagas, as well as Siberian kale. The species classification of rutabagas is a bit confused among various authorities, but they shouldn't interbreed with species of turnips you'll be growing. Again, to maintain genetic diversity, grow at least six plants but preferably a dozen.

Despite these differences, seed saving for all three is the same. In areas with mild winters, you can heavily mulch the roots in the ground to help them survive over the winter. In areas with harsh winters, the roots should be dug, foliage trimmed to two inches, and stored in peat moss at 95 percent humidity and temperatures between 33 and 40 degrees. In the spring, plant them in the ground at their original depth as soon as the soil can be worked.

The bulbs will leaf out and then grow a stalk around three feet tall. This stalk is somewhat delicate, and I would recommend staking it. An amazing number of flowers will grow on the stalk, and bees will seemingly congregate from miles around to have fun spreading pollen and fertilizing the plants. Harvest the seed-pods once they turn brown. As they are fragile, I recommend stripping the pods into a plastic bag. The pods can then be broken up and the seed separated from the chafe through winnowing.

Let the seed set out in an open bowl for a couple of weeks and then dry over a desiccant for a week before storing in a sealed container for up to five years in a cool, dark place.

Preparation and Preservation

Due to tradition, we think of rutabagas, and turnips as something only eaten cooked and radishes as something only eaten raw. The reality is that these are interchangeable. Likewise, we eat turnip greens but neglect radish greens, which are just as edible and delicious. Rutabaga greens are likewise edible. The greens, if dry, will keep in a bag in the refrigerator for a week. They can be steam-blanched for four minutes and then chilled in ice water, dried, and frozen in freezer bags from which all air has been excluded. Or they can be dehydrated after blanching and used as an addition to soups, stews, dips and sauces.

The roots store best in peat or sand with the leaves removed at 95 percent humidity and temperatures of 32 to 35 degrees. Summer radishes will keep for a month like this, but turnips, winter radishes, and rutabagas will keep for several months this way.

In practice, it is hard to achieve such perfect storage conditions, which is why you will often find turnips and rutabagas in the supermarket that have been waxed. The wax prevents moisture loss for storage in less humid environments, and because the hot wax kills pathogens on the surface, it allows for long-term storage under less perfect conditions. To wax turnips and rutabagas, remove the tops and thoroughly wash and dry them first. (They must be thoroughly dried before immersing in wax or dangerous splatters of wax will occur.) Heat up regular canning wax in a pot on an electric stove or using a double boiler if you have a gas stove. Using a slotted spoon, dip the vegetable in the wax and make sure it is thoroughly wet with the wax; then set aside on some paper bags for the wax to harden.

Don't hold vegetable in the wax any longer than necessary to thoroughly coat it with wax. Peel the wax and top layer of the vegetable and discard before eating.

Radishes, rutabagas, and turnips also freeze well. Cut into uniform half-inch chunks, water blanch for four minutes or steam blanch for six minutes, cool thoroughly in ice water for another five minutes, pat dry, and then seal in freezer bags excluding air. You could also opt to dehydrate them for future use in soups or stews by following the directions of the manufacturer of your dehydrator.

There are a lot of ways to eat turnips and rutabagas. They can be boiled and mashed like potatoes, baked, cooked into stews, and more. The greens can be eaten raw in salads, steamed, or boiled in the fashion of collard greens. I like to sauté them with olive oil and garlic.

Oven-Roasted Radishes
Ingredients:

    1 lb radishes, cut uniformly in halves or quartered
    1 leek (mild onion can be substituted)
    1 tbsp toasted sesame seed oil
    1 tbsp canola oil
    2 tbsp soy sauce

⊗ Oven roasted radishes will have you looking at radishes in a whole new light!

Procedure:

Preheat oven to 425 degrees. Wash and dry the radishes and cut into uniform sections so they bake at approximately the same rate. Thoroughly coat the radishes with the toasted sesame seed oil and canola oil by mixing with your hands in a bowl, and pour into a baking dish. Put in the oven and set your timer for 20 minutes. Thinly slice the white portion of the leek, discarding the remainder. When the timer goes off, add the leeks and soy sauce to the radishes and mix thoroughly; then return to the oven for another 7 minutes. You'll never think of radishes as just a salad garnish again.

19

Permaculture with Perennial Vegetables

As described in *Mini Farming*, plantings of berry canes, fruit or nut trees, and grapevines are all a form of permaculture. Though such plantings require some degree of maintenance, overall they require very little time, effort, and money for the amount of food derived. Unfortunately, most vegetables planted in the garden need to be replanted every year. This entails a great deal of time and effort.

A little-known fact is that most of the vegetables that we plant as annuals for purposes of efficiency and high yield are derived from wild ancestors that are perennial. These wild ancestors are far less susceptible to pests and diseases than their domesticated progeny and therefore don't require the degree of crop rotation that would otherwise be needed to maintain a healthy crop. It wouldn't be practical to grow perennial vegetables exclusively, but it is entirely practical to dedicate three, four, or more beds to selected perennials because of the savings in time and effort.

For example, rather than growing kale (which is grown as an annual), you could grow sea kale. Sea kale is perennial and will return year after year. Sea kale is not only perfectly edible, it was featured in Thomas Jefferson's garden and contains all of the familiar nutrition of cabbage family plants. In addition, as long as the pH is adjusted to higher than 6 to avoid clubroot, sea kale will never experience a serious pest or disease problem.

Sea kale is just one example of how you can grow perennial vegetables that were an important part of our diet until very modern times, while saving a tremendous amount of time and effort in the long run. There are many vegetables that if handled correctly can constitute more or less permanent plantings. When a bed is dedicated to this sort of crop, it is taken out of availability for other vegetables but requires far less time and effort to maintain.

I have already covered asparagus in an earlier chapter. If properly prepared initially, asparagus beds can remain productive for decades. If you keep the bed weeded and harvest prudently, you'll have plenty of asparagus every year without ever having to put shovel to soil. The same applies to the herbs discussed in the chapter on herbs—many of them will return every year either due to their perennial nature or from self-reseeding. Examples include mints, balms, sage, and thyme, among others. My mini farm has two 4 ft. x 8 ft. beds dedicated strictly to culinary and medicinal herbs and another 4 ft. x 8 ft. bed that produces impressive quantities of asparagus. Though I rotate where I plant annual herbs year to year, my herb beds require less maintenance than any of the others.

You aren't limited to sea kale, asparagus, and herbs, however. There are a number of other vegetables that make an excellent choice for permanent plantings in raised beds.

Soil Preparation and Care

In general, the beds for perennials need to be prepared just as you would prepare for any other crop by correcting for nutrient deficiencies, adding micro-nutrients, correcting the pH, and incorporating plenty of organic matter. Because perennial vegetables by definition remain in that bed a long time, you should make sure you incorporate at least eight cubic feet of compost per 4 ft. x 8 ft. bed.

When planting more typical crops, you have the opportunity to directly incorporate additional nutrients and compost annually via admixture, whereas you don't have this luxury with perennials because such disturbance of the soil could harm or kill the plants.

The good news is that most perennial vegetables put nowhere near the strain on soil as their annual and biennial cousins, so they require less fertilizer. In fact, a properly prepared bed may, in some cases, require no amendments at all for several years thereafter. This is another good reason why establishing a few beds of perennial vegetables makes sense.

At least every year, compost should be added to the beds. You can't turn it in, so just spread it as evenly as you can on top. I prefer that it be added twice annually: once in the fall and then again in the spring. After a while, you'll be able to judge how much compost is needed just by digging up a bit of soil and looking, but a good guideline is you'll need three cubic feet annually per 4 ft. x 8 ft. bed. The winter weather helps to break down the compost added in fall, and the famous April showers will help incorporate both that and the compost added in early spring.

The compost should be well finished so that it won't leach nutrients. If you find that your compost particles are too big to spread effectively, you can use a piece of half-inch hardware cloth to strain your compost. Put the pieces that don't fit through the holes back into the pile and use the smaller pieces for spreading.

You should use a soil test kit to test your beds for nitrogen, phosphorus, and potassium annually. If a perennial bed requires the addition of one or more of these, you should thoroughly mix the needed amount with the compost you will be adding. You should make sure to also add micronutrients to the compost that you spread on the beds. This could take the form of kelp solids, sea solids, some Celtic Sea Salt (no more than six ounces per 4 ft. x 8 ft. bed annually), or some wood ash, among other sources. These will get leached into the bed via rain and weather, as well as by the action of earthworms and other soil organisms.

Weeds are the greatest enemy of perennial vegetables because, unlike your annual beds that you can aggressively hoe or flame or from which every living green thing can be removed before planting cover crops, perennial plants can't be disturbed like that and survive.

An ounce of prevention will get your beds off to a good start. As most perennial vegetables are planted in early summer, you have ample opportunity to pre-sprout and remove as many weeds as possible. Just let the weeds sprout in the bed, and then hoe them. You can do this several times in the spring before time to plant. Then, just before planting, flame the bed thoroughly to kill any seeds in the top one-quarter inch of soil.

Once you have planted, you will have to hand-weed the beds in most cases, though there may be some instances when you can use a stirrup hoe. A stirrup hoe only disturbs the top quarter to half inch of soil and so will do the least damage to the root systems of desired plants. In the fall, when plants die back, you can also mulch to create a barrier that will keep new seeds from falling into the beds and prevent many that are already in the bed from sprouting. You can use shredded leaves or shredded straw as a mulch, but you should make sure to remove it in the spring so it doesn't inhibit the emergence of desired crops.

⊗ The onions on the right are perennial potato onions. They are smaller, but delicious.

Onions

The standard bulbing onion discussed in an earlier chapter is planted annually, but if you are willing to deal with smaller bulbs, there are several varieties of onion that divide into clusters of onions underground and regrow every year. These include Welsh onion, garlic chives, potato onions, walking onions, and shallots.

I maintain a bed of potato onions. Late every summer when they die back, I pull the clusters of onions and replant about 15 percent of them equally spaced around that bed to grow back the next year. This way I have an infinite supply of small onions that go great in stews, and the amount of work I have to invest is minimal.

These onions are smallish but have vastly superior flavor to the standard bulbing onions. Once you have used these in a stew, you'll see why so many pioneers carried these with them for their homesteads out West.

Garlic as a Perennial

Garlic is most often grown as an annual, but once you have established a bed of garlic, it can be grown as a perennial. Before you plant the bulbs in fall, make sure you till in a good quantity of finished compost—at least four cubic feet per 4 ft. x 8 ft. bed. Then make sure to add micronutrients. After that, use the techniques covered in the chapter on onions, such as presprouting to reduce weed problems, as much as possible. Then, plant your bulbs at a six-inch spacing in all directions.

In early summer, many of the plants will form blossoms. Pinch off the shoots once they are a couple of feet tall so the plants will form bulbs. (You can collect them earlier and fry them up as garlic scapes.) Harvest the bulbs from the large plants in the late summer, and let the smaller plants die back. The next year, those smaller plants will sprout.

The biggest problem you will have in such a planting is weeds. I recommend mulching in the fall with dead leaves you rake off the yard. These leaves will compost over time and enrich the soil, and they will prevent many weeds as well. Come spring, if they haven't rotted down enough to let the garlic sprout, gently remove them. You can control weeds the rest of the season with a carefully used stirrup hoe.

Jerusalem Artichokes

A friend in Connecticut introduced me to Jerusalem artichokes several years ago, and I have maintained a bed of them ever since. Jerusalem artichokes are an indigenous root vegetable that is high in an indigestible starch called inulin. You'll find special pastas for diabetics made using inulin in some stores.

Jerusalem artichokes are propagated by ordering some tubers and planting them in a bed in the spring. In the fall, you will harvest about twenty times as many tubers as you originally planted. This will continue year after year ad infinitum. In fact, if you aren't vigilant, they will invade and take over your entire yard!

Jerusalem artichokes are usually thoroughly scrubbed, boiled, and then either sliced or mashed and served with butter. In this form, they are delicious. If you have never eaten them before, just eat a little bit the first few times because your large intestine likely lacks sufficient numbers of the bacteria needed to process inulin. This lack of bacteria will cause diarrhea. If you eat a little at a time and build up to it, you'll soon find that you can pack away a whole plate of these delicious roots without any trouble at all.

Groundnut (*Apios americana*)

I have included the scientific name of this plant because there are several plants called "groundnut" that might be confused. This groundnut is a member of the same family as fava beans. It is a perennial vine native to the United States. During

the regular growing season, it grows a bean vine that bears numerous bean pods. These pods can be harvested young as green beans or allowed to ripen into dried beans. Over the course of the season the vines store up energy in the tubers, from which the groundnut will resprout for the next season indefinitely. The tubers are likewise edible and unusually rich in protein for a root vegetable.

Scorzonera or Black Salsify

Common salsify or oyster plant (*Tragopogon porrifolius*) is a biennial root crop (which is well worth growing, incidentally), but the closely related scorzonera (*Scorzonera hispanica*) is perennial. Common salsify roots should be harvested in their first year because, once the plant flowers in its second year, the roots become unappetizing and the plant dies. Scorzonera, however, can be grown year after year. The roots of scorzonera are typically thin but can grow as long as three feet, making harvest difficult. Growing it as a perennial, you can get thicker roots that have more food plus are less likely to break by waiting until the second year to harvest. Meanwhile, simply allow it to make flowers and seeds as it wishes, and the bed will be liberally reseeded to replenish those plants that you harvest.

The black skin of the roots is inedible and needs to be removed. When you remove it, though, the white flesh almost immediately turns black. To prevent this, have a bowl of water with salt or lemon juice mixed in and throw the roots in there as soon as they are peeled. Scorzonera is usually boiled and served with other vegetables. I prefer to blanch it (and salsify), dehydrate, and serve in winter stews.

Good King Henry

Good King Henry is a perennial relative of amaranth that is native to Europe. It is planted from seed the first year. Thereafter, each spring the new shoots are blanched and eaten like asparagus, and a few leaves are harvested throughout the summer and prepared like spinach.

This mulched scorzonera produces abundantly with little effort. **»**

Perennial Broccoli

Perennial broccoli is a form of broccoli that, instead of forming a head, sends up slender stalks with just a few flowers on each. The entire slender stalk is cut and eaten. Perennial broccoli is transplanted in late summer. In northern areas such as New Hampshire, it will need to be overwintered in a high tunnel or similar environment, but no such care is required south of Maryland. Once overwintered, it starts sending up stalks in the spring. These stalks can be harvested until the next winter when the plant is overwintered again. Three high-yielding varieties of perennial broccoli are Nine Star, Red Arrow, and Bordeaux.

Rhubarb

Rhubarb was once so valuable in Europe that its cost was four times that of saffron and almost three times that of opium.[1] Luckily, you can grow it for yourself at trivial cost. In warmer parts of the country, rhubarb will grow year-round, but in colder zones it will die back during the winter and re-emerge in spring. The leaves

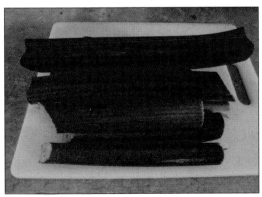

are poisonous both due to a high concentration of oxalic acid and the likely presence of an anthraquinone glycoside. (This is a drastic purgative, for which purpose rhubarb was

« An embarrassment of riches, this rhubarb is destined for a strawberry-rhubarb dessert.

---

1 Lloyd, J. (1921) *Origin and History of all the Pharmacopeial Vegetable Drugs, Chemicals and Preparations with Bibliography*, p. 270

used in medicine.) The concentration of oxalic acid in rhubarb stalks, however, is so low as to be harmless.

Rhubarb stalks taste highly acidic, but almost all of this is from malic acid—the same acid that gives green apples their tartness. Rhubarb should be started indoors from seeds in the spring, transplanted in early summer, and then allowed to over-winter. You can harvest up to half the stalks each year. Just gently pull them from the plant and strip the green matter of the leaves from them.

Sea Kale

I mentioned sea kale in the introduction to this chapter because it is such an excellent example of a perennial vegetable. It is tasty, nutritious, and can grow anywhere in the continental United States. It should be started indoors and then transplanted in early summer. Germination can take as long as five weeks but can be accelerated a bit if you make several shallow nicks in the seed coating with a sharp knife and soak in water overnight before sowing.

It should be transplanted into deeply worked, very rich soil that is high in organic matter. Because its origin is near the sea, it will particularly benefit from the use of trace minerals in the form of unrefined sea salt. Add about six ounces of unrefined sea salt (for example, Celtic Sea Salt) annually to the bed. Its first shoots can be harvested and treated like asparagus, but its leaves and stalks can be eaten year-round.

Watercress

Closely related to annual garden cress, watercress is a reliable perennial that is one of the oldest leaf vegetables known to have been eaten by humans. It is rich in numerous essential vitamins and is a proven cancer fighter.

Because it is semiaquatic and will whither and die in still water, it can be difficult to maintain suitable conditions for its culture in most gardens. However, it is in sufficient demand that it might be worthwhile to set up a dedicated area.

Watercress can be easily grown using the inexpensive white two-gallon buckets, a kiddie pool, and a small pond aerator. Drill several holes in the bottom of each bucket and fill the bottom half with gravel. Marble chips would be ideal as watercress prefers its water to be slightly alkaline, and marble is simply a super-compressed form of lime that dissolves very slowly. Then fill the container the rest of the way with rich garden soil. Set the containers in the kiddie pool, fill the pool with six inches of water, and make sure to run the pond aerator for at least four hours a day. Change the water completely once a week. Once freezing weather arrives, empty the kiddie pool, and store your containers of cress in an unheated outside area until spring.

Wood Nettle (*Laportea canadensis*)

I've listed the scientific name so there's no misunderstanding the plant I'm describing. Don't confuse wood nettle with horse nettle. Horse nettle is an unrelated plant, all the parts of which are poisonous. Wood nettle is a perennial plant usually found in moist woodlands in dappled shade. Wood nettle is a monoecious herb that has separate male and female flowers on the same plant. Not only will wood nettles reseed themselves from the fruits they develop from the upper female flowers, but they will also spread through their root system.

If you have an area of your lawn that only gets a couple of hours of sun daily but is shaded the rest of the time, wood nettle can be an ideal solution for making that area productive. If you can't find wood nettle seeds, stinging nettle (*Urtica dioica*) will work just as well in these conditions and is just as tasty.

Start the seeds by storing in the freezer for six weeks and then planting them in well-watered peat pots three months before last frost. Transplant at a spacing of one foot into your bed. Water the bed about twice as often as you water your other beds.

Eating a plant that wants to sting you as self-defense is a bit tricky. Wood nettle is covered with hairs, and some of those hairs are hypodermic syringes that inject a mixture of formic acid, histamine, and acetylcholine, among other compounds. Formic acid and histamine in particular will make it sting. The juice of jewelweed will cure the rash, but it is best avoided altogether by handling the fresh plant with heavy gloves. Once collected, strip the leaves from the stem, and sauté or steam them. The cooking process softens the needles so they can't sting and inactivates the chemicals. You'll be surprised at how delicious they are, as well as rich in vitamins and minerals.

⊗ Wood nettles can be grown in beds and are also found in the wild.

Index of Recipes

Alphabetical Index

B

B vitamins, 51, 89, 169
Bacillus subtilis, 78, 108-109, 151
Bacillus thuringiensis, 45, 66
Bacterial inoculants, 27
Bacterial leaf spot, 135-136
Bacterial wilt disease, 74, 76, 78, 108, 162
Baked Cauliflower, 48-49
Baking soda, 46, 78, 109, 160
Basil, 93-94
Bean beetles, 28-29
Beans, 25-33
Beer, 85
Beets, 33-41
Benign prostatic hyperplasia, 158
Beta carotene, 34, 51
Black Crowder Cowpea, 126
Black leg, 46, 150
Black rot, 46
Black Salsify, 198
Black Turtle, Dry Bush, 27, 30
Black-eyed peas, 26
Blood meal, 7, 19, 64, 106, 172
Blossom end rot, 159, 163, 171-172
Blue Lake, Green Pole, 26
Bonemeal, 19, 34, 117, 135
Borage, 94-95
Borax, 14, 34, 186
Boron, 6, 12-14, 42-43, 146, 186
Botrytis, 4, 20, 119-120
Botulism, 97, 180
BPH, 158

Broccoli, x, xii, 5, 14, 41-49, 65, 87, 119, 184, 187, 188, 199,
Bt, 45
Bull's Blood, 34
Butter Lemon Asparagus, 23

C

Cabbage, 41-49, 84-85, 99, 151, 184, 186-188, 194
Cabbage loopers, 44-45
Cabbage maggots, 186
Cabbage root maggots, 45, 187
Caffeine, 85
Calcium, 89, 121, 163, 171, 184
Calcium chloride, 9
Cancer, 41, 84, 87-88, 105, 113, 158, 169, 177, 184, 200
Cantaloupes, 106-107
Capsaicin, 133-134, 139
Carbofuran, 149
Carbon, 89
Carbon dioxide, 69
Carrion beetles, 35
Carrot flies, 55-56
Carrots, 51-59, 74, 86, 100, 125, 131, 149,
Casaba, 106
Cauliflower, 41-49
Certified Seed Potatoes, 146-147, 153
Chantenay, 52
Chard, 83, 84, 159
Cheese, xvi
Cheesecloth, 178
Cherry tomatoes, 170, 177
Chervil, 84, 89
Chives, 95, 196
Chlorpicrin, 149

Cholesterol, 177
Chromium, 12
Cilantro, 70-71, 95-96
Citric acid, 98, 179
Citrullus lanatus, 106,
Click beetles, 55
Clubroot, 45, 187, 194
Cobalt, 12
Coffee grounds, 85,
Colorado potato beetles, 148-149
Compost, 4-5, 10-15, 19-21, 27, 34, 42, 45, 52, 57, 64, 66, 74, 84, 106, 116, 119-121, 126, 129, 135, 138-139, 146, 150, 152, 159, 163, 171-172, 174, 186, 187, 194-197
Composting, 4-5, 10-15, 28, 46, 76, 128, 162
Copper, 6, 12-13, 136, 151, 161-162, 183-184
Copper sulfate, 161
Coriander, 70, 95, 141
Corn, 61-72
Corn earworm, 65-66
Corn salad, 83, 86
Coronary artery disease, 33
Crenshaw, 106
Cress, 83, 88, 201
Crop rotation, xv, 4, 11-12, 15, 27, 29, 44, 54, 76, 77, 85, 119, 121, 128, 136, 138, 148, 150, 151, 161, 171, 174-175, 187, 193
Crossbreeding, 47-48
Crowns, 18-19, 21, 45,
Cucumber beetles, 74-78, 108, 160-162
Cucumber mosaic, 162

Squash vine borers, 75, 162

Stirrup hoe, 44, 65, 128, 136, 160, 196-197

Straw, 4, 20, 36, 97, 119, 196

Strontium, 12-13

Sugar, 22, 39, 49, 52, 58, 62-63, 67-68, 106, 110-111, 123, 126-127, 129-131, 141, 144, 167, 175, 180-181

Sugar snap, 126-127, 129-131

Sugarbaby, 106

Sugary Enhanced, 62, 63

Sulfur, 7-8, 10, 12, 117, 174

Sulfur coated urea, 7

Summer squash, 157-158, 160, 163-165, 167

Supersweet, 62

Surround, 55, 108, 129,

Sweet corn, 62-63, 67-70, 165,

Symbiotic, 4, 127

T

Tarragon, 101-102

Thermometer, 53, 136-137

Thermophilically, 152

Thiamine, 183

Thrips, 120-121

Thyme, 93-94, 102-103, 194

Tobacco, 10-11, 138, 144, 174-175

Tomatine, 177

Tomato hornworms, 95, 173

Tomato russet mite, 174

Tomatoes, x, xii, 5, 11, 18, 65, 70, 73, 95, 138, 150-151, 167, 169-181

Top Crop, Green Bush, 27

Trace minerals, 11, 19, 74, 84, 121, 186, 200

Trellis, xv, 28, 74-76, 107, 126-127, 151, 159-160, 170-171, 175

True botanical seed, 146-147

True potato seed, 153

True seed, 144, 146-147, 153

Turnips, 183-190

U

Umbel, 57-58

Urea, 172

USDA Germplasm Repository, 153

V

Verticillium, 145, 174-175

Vidalia, 115, 117

Vinegar, 22, 38, 48-49, 58, 97, 102-103, 111, 122-123, 141, 180-181

Vitamin A, 73, 87, 89, 133, 183

Vitamin B1, 158

Vitamin B6, 133, 143, 158,

Vitamin C, 34, 51, 73, 87, 89, 122, 125, 133, 143, 158, 183-184

Vitamin E, 51, 184

Vitamin K, 33, 51, 87, 89, 90, 125, 183,

Vitamins, 12, 17, 33, 41, 51, 84-89, 105, 110, 169, 200-201

W

Waltham 29, 42

Watercress, 83, 88, 200

Waterlogged, 8, 18, 44, 137,

Watermelon, 105-111

Weeds, 4, 19-20, 28-29, 35, 43-46, 53-56, 65, 75, 107-108, 118, 127-128, 135-138, 147, 150, 159-160, 172, 187, 195-197

Wet feet, 18, 137

Whiteflies, 172-173

Wine, 103, 170, 179

Wine vinegar, 103

Winnowing, 30, 37, 58, 87, 189

Winter squash, xv, 157-160, 163-165

Wireworms, 4, 54-56, 128, 148-150

Wood ash, 19, 195

Wood ashes, 6, 11, 14, 34, 52, 56, 117, 186

Wood nettle, 201

Z

Zeaxanthin, 34,

Zinc, 12-13, 158

Zucchini, 157-159, 164, 167